STUDIES IN RUSSIA AND EAST EUROPE
formerly Studies in Russian and East European History

Chairman of the Editorial Board: M.A. Branch, Director, School of Slavonic and East European Studies.

This series includes books on general, political, historical, economic, social and cultural themes relating to Russia and East Europe written or edited by members of the School of Slavonic and East European Studies in the University of London, or by authors working in association with the School. Titles already published are listed below. Further titles are in preparation.

D.G. Kirby (*editor*)
FINLAND AND RUSSIA, 1808–1920: Documents

Michael Kirkwood (*editor*)
LANGUAGE PLANNING IN THE SOVIET UNION

Paul Latawski (*editor*)
THE RECONSTRUCTION OF POLAND, 1914–23

Martin McCauley
THE RUSSIAN REVOLUTION AND THE SOVIET STATE, 1917–1921:
    DOCUMENTS (*editor*)

KHRUSHCHEV AND THE DEVELOPMENT OF SOVIET AGRICULTURE

COMMUNIST POWER IN EUROPE: 1914–1949 (*editor*)

MARXISM-LENINISM IN THE GERMAN DEMOCRATIC REPUBLIC: THE
    SOCIALIST UNITY PARTY (SED)

THE GERMAN DEMOCRATIC REPUBLIC SINCE 1945

KHRUSCHEV AND KHRUSHCHEVISM (*editor*)

THE SOVIET UNION UNDER GORBACHEV (*editor*)

GORBACHEV AND *PERESTROIKA* (*editor*)

Martin McCauley and Stephen Carter (*editors*)
LEADERSHIP AND SUCCESSION IN THE SOVIET UNION, EASTERN
    EUROPE AND CHINA

Martin McCauley and Peter Waldron
THE EMERGENCE OF THE MODERN RUSSIAN STATE, 1856–81

Arnold McMillin (*editor*)
FROM PUSHKIN TO *PALISANDRIIA*
UNDER EASTERN EYES: The West as Reflected in Recent Russian Émigré
    Writing

Evan Mawdsley
THE RUSSIAN REVOLUTION AND THE BALTIC FLEET

Laszló Péter and Robert B. Pynsent (*editors*)
INTELLECTUALS AND THE FUTURE IN THE HABSBURG MONARCHY,
    1890–1914

Robert B. Pynsent
T.G. MASARYK (1850–1937) Volume 2: Thinker and Critic (*editor*)

MODERN SLOVAK PROSE: Fiction Since 1954

Ian W. Roberts
NICHOLAS I AND THE RUSSIAN INTERVENTION IN HUNGARY

Keith Sword (*editor*)
THE SOVIET TAKEOVER OF THE POLISH EASTERN PROVINCES,
    1939–41

J.J. Tomiak (*editor*)
WESTERN PERSPECTIVES ON SOVIET EDUCATION IN THE 1980s

Paul I. Trensky
THE FICTION OF JOSEF ŠKVORECKÝ

Stephen White and Alex Pravda (*editors*)
IDEOLOGY AND SOVIET POLITICS

Stanley B. Winters (*editor*)
T.G. MASARYK (1850–1937) Volume 1: Thinker and Politician

Alan Wood and R.A. French (*editors*)
THE DEVELOPMENT OF SIBERIA: People and Resources

Under Eastern Eyes

The West as Reflected in Recent Russian Émigré Writing

Edited by Arnold McMillin

Professor of Russian Literature
School of Slavonic and East European Studies
University of London

in association with the
School of Slavonic and East European Studies
University of London

First published 1991 by
MACMILLAN ACADEMIC AND PROFESSIONAL LTD
Houndmills, Basingstoke, Hampshire RG21 2XS
and London
Companies and representatives
throughout the world

ISBN 0–333–55041–2 hardcover

A catalogue record for this book is available
from the British Library.

Printed in Hong Kong

Contents

Notes on the Contributors

Vasilii Aksenov, the celebrated Russian novelist, left the Soviet Union in 1980 and is now a professor at George Mason University in the United States. His works are translated into many languages and almost all are available in English.

Galina Belaia works at the Institute of World Literature in Moscow and is a professor at Moscow State University. Author of numerous books and articles on Russian literature and society.

Nora Buhks lectures on Russian literature at the Sorbonne. Author of many articles on Russian literature and the Soviet media. Her book *Le Journalisme de la Péréstroika. Les Techniques du Renouvement* came out in 1989.

Anatolii Gladilin, the Russian writer, has lived in Paris since 1976. He is author of ten books published in the Soviet Union and six published in the West, several of which have been translated into various languages. *The Making and Unmaking of a Soviet Writer* (1979) exists only in English.

Julian Graffy lectures in Russian Language and Literature at the School of Slavonic and East European Studies, University of London. Recent publications include translations of V.E. Maksimov's *Ark for the Uncalled* and of the correspondence between Maiakovskii and Lily Brik.

Michael Kirkwood is a Senior Lecturer in Russian Language at the School of Slavonic and East European Studies, University of London. He has co-edited (with Philip Hanson) *Alexander Zinoviev as Writer and Thinker* and is the editor of, and a contributor to, *Language Planning in the Soviet Union*.

Lev Loseff, the distinguished Russian poet, is a professor at Dartmouth College, New Hampshire, and the author of many books and articles on modern Russian literature.

Arnold McMillin is Professor of Russian Literature in the University of London. He has published widely on Russian and Byelorussian literature.

Robert Porter is a Senior Lecturer in Russian at Bristol University. His books include *Understanding Soviet Politics through Literature* (with Martin Crouch) (1984) and *Four Contemporary Russian Writers* (1989).

Hans Rothe is Professor of Russian in the University of Bonn. Erstwhile President of the Modern Humanities Research Association, he is author of many books and articles on Russian literature and history.

Gerald Smith is Professor of Russian in the University of Oxford and Fellow of New College. He has published widely on eighteenth- and twentieth-century Russian literature.

Zinovii Zinik's prose written since emigration from Moscow in 1975 examines different aspects of the 'doubleness and duplicity' of émigré existence. Among his recently translated novels are *The Mushroom Picker* (1988) and *The Lord and the Gamekeeper* (1991); the latter is expected to be published in the Soviet Union shortly.

Introduction

Time moves quickly nowadays. Place, on the other hand, is more stable, though it might well be asked whether the present-day citizens of Leipzig feel they are in the same place when part of the GDR as in the Fourth Reich. History, it seems, has never moved faster, and nowhere, perhaps, is this more the case than in Russia and Eastern Europe. One minor natural consequence of such entirely welcome developments is the great difficulty of writing anything that will not be out of date before the ink dries. Indeed, the very lively and successful conference from which papers in this volume have been selected might have provoked less vigorous discussion if in September 1989 *perestroika* had really found wings, as it was to do some few months later. That said, the theme of the conference – and of this volume – remains one of great interest, for the Third-Wave Russian writers are, with very few exceptions, still living in the West, and their reactions to life there throws considerable light on Soviet mentality, on the psychology of nationalism and emigration (the latter not substantially changed since the days of Ovid), and, not least, on our own societies and attitudes, observed and depicted with far more acuity than was brought to their task by Conrad's characters.

The main flood of the Third Wave of emigration occurred between 1973 and 1981, as a result of Mr Brezhnev's opportunistic policy of releasing a number of Jews, ostensibly to travel to Israel, and expelling or forcing to emigrate many writers, artists and musicians whose non-conformist activities he deemed too much of a nuisance to tolerate. Disastrous as this semi-enforced exodus was for Soviet literature and, indeed, for Soviet culture as a whole, it did afford new opportunities to many writers either to begin new careers or to develop, without the constraints of censorship, careers already well established before their expatriation.

A particularly welcome feature of the conference was the opportunity for exiled Russian writers to discuss their work and aspects of emigration with Western scholars. And added spice and vitality were provided by the participation of Galina Belaia, a professor at Moscow University, who spoke frankly about contemporary attitudes in the Soviet Union, many of which were all too clearly reflected in the different camps of the Third Wave of emigration, most notably the

'authoritarian-nationalist' and the 'liberal-democratic'. Amongst the
writers in attendance were Vasilii Aksenov, in the 1960s probably the
most popular of all young Soviet writers, and now one of the most
successful of the Third-Wave expatriates at coping with the West – he
alone has written a book specifically devoted to his new environment
in America. A fellow writer of Aksenov in the Youth Prose movement, Anatolii Gladilin, has, likewise, continued to write entertain-
ingly in the West. He shares with Aksenov the debatable honour of
both writing in his own name and being written about in this volume.
Zinovii Zinik, who lived in Israel before settling in Britain, is author
of a number of novels that throw a not always flattering light on his
adopted countries, as well as a splendidly thought-provoking essay on
emigration for this volume; Lev Loseff, himself a distinguished poet
as well as critic, appears here in the latter capacity, writing about Iosif
Brodskii, a poet who, like Aksenov in prose (though neither would
welcome the comparison), felt the West in his intellectual and
spiritual blood long before he left Russia.

The writers mentioned and the books discussed here represent only
a tiny proportion of the total possible: by 1982 Olga Matich had
counted over 100 expatriate writers,[1] and – taking into account the
new Russian writers in the West, some entirely ephemeral – I have
myself on file at least 200 names, whilst between 1977 and 1984
Gerald Smith noted 163 separate volumes of Russian verse published
in the West. The writers on whom this volume focuses are none the
less representative of many other strands of Russian literature
abroad, and reflect many other writers' attitudes to their new Western environment. Such attitudes vary widely. At one extreme (the
word is decidedly inappropriate when referring to such a sane and
balanced writer) is Vasilii Aksenov's contention that 'emigration is
the best condition for [Russian] literature'[2] and his absorption by the
(not necessarily negative) phenomenon of American provincialism.
Of course, a very different view of America is given in Eduard
Limonov's violently exhibitionistic novel *Eto ia – Edichka*. Also poles
apart from Aksenov's calm acceptance of his new life is Aleksandr
Zinov'ev's view of emigration as slow torture, leading to a miserable
death, perhaps not dissimilar to that of the characters in his novel
Ziiaiushchie vysoty who 'voluntarily' enter a cremation chamber accompanied by an injunction seemingly intended to sum up Ibanskian
and émigré life in equal measure: 'As you leave, take the urn
containing your ashes with you!'.[3]

Emigration may, indeed, be an unhappy lot, though comparison of

Orlova with Poppe reminds us that misery and complaints are far
from inevitable. In a very interesting essay, 'Emigration as a Literary
Device'[4] Zinovii Zinik has compared an émigré's life to that of a
long-sentence prisoner, a survivor of a shipwreck on a desert island,
or a ghost's existence in a lonely Gothic castle, and in his novel
Russofobka i fungofil a KGB-sponsored accident is described as
'lending a little much-needed spice to the lives of émigrés bored with
living in freedom'.[5] At worst an émigré may be reduced to King
Lear's 'unaccommodated man who is no more but such a poor bare
forked animal'. In such picturesque assessments the imaginative
melodrama of exile has replaced the often traumatic drama that
preceded it, and realistic self-assessment becomes a rare, perhaps
irrelevant, commodity. However, the ex-Soviet journalist and writer
Sergei Dovlatov, replying to a questionnaire, put the phenomenon of
emigration into an unusually rational perspective when he wrote, 'A
human being does not change, and the forms of life remain as they
have been. We simply exchange some sorrows for others. That's all.
For myself, I definitely prefer the sorrows here'.[6] Meanwhile the
expatriate writers continue to produce interesting literature in their
new surroundings, and almost none of them, or, indeed, of any other
members of the intelligentsia, show a serious desire to go back to
Russia, whatever the blandishments, and whatever the sometimes
hypocritical statements some of them make to the Soviet media;
meanwhile a grossly misleading picture of unrelieved émigré misery
continues to be presented in conservative Soviet fiction. In Iaroslav
Shipov's story 'Uezdnyi chudotvorets', for instance, a local medical
assistant, having been offered the chance to work as a doctor in Paris,
says, 'What sort of life would that be? To suffer, go through torments, endure insults. And then to end with an absurd and empty
death.'[7]

Traditional Russian *toska* or nostalgia notwithstanding, the writers
represented in this volume reflect a wide range of émigré experience
and present a view of Western life that varies from traditional, at
times predictable, to the downright startling, be it at the level of
politics, sociology or ethnopsychology. Without the Third Wave of
emigration the development of *glasnost'* in the Soviet Union could
never have proceeded as rapidly as it did, and the present policy of
publishing many Third-Wave writers in Soviet journals is advancing
the metropolitan literary process at a remarkable speed. The view of
the West presented by these literary works will help equally to correct
idealisation and to offset propaganda-induced prejudice (the latter,

remarkably, still not dead in the Soviet Union, despite widespread cynicism at anything emanating from the authorities). It will also tell us much about the individual writers and, not least interesting, about ourselves and the way we live.

Arnold McMillin
London, September 1990

NOTES

1. Olga Matich and Michael Henry Heim (eds), *The Third Wave: Russian Literature in Emigration* (Ann Arbor, Michigan, 1984), p. 20.
2. Vasilii Aksenov, 'Luchshee sostoianie literatury – emigratsiia', *Sem' dnei*, 50 (1984), pp. 21–4.
3. Aleksandr Zinov'ev, *Ziiaiushchie vysoty* (Lausanne, 1976), p. 828.
4. *Lovely Jobbly*, I, 1 (1990), pp. 42–5.
5. Zinovii Zinik, *Russofobka i fungofil* (London, 1984), p. 253.
6. *Humanities in Society*, VII, 3–4 (1984), p. 232.
7. *Nash sovremennik*, no. 4, 1989, p. 122.

1 Sick Ideas of a Sick Society: The 'West-East' Theme in Soviet and Émigré Criticism

Galina Belaia

Before embarking on the main theme, I should like to make a few preliminary observations. If one recalls the old Russian arguments on the 'West-East' theme, it is impossible not to notice that they always became more intense at Russia's moments of historical crisis. Thus it was in the 1840s to the 1860s, and thus also during the October Revolution. This insistent turning to the 'West-East' theme, which usually figures in the alternative form of 'West *or* East', has always concealed within itself dissatisfaction with the present and thoughts about Russia's possible paths in the future.

This connection between our theme and the turning points of Russian history continues today, and it is precisely because of these links that the objective scholarly study of the 'West-East' question has always been hampered by political considerations. The interests of the moment and collective passions have distorted the problem, replacing it with a retrospective review of history and intellectual forecasts of the future of Russia: orientated either on its remaining true to its messianic mission or on its repeating (with a certain historical delay) the path of western civilisation.

Looking at contemporary Russia from the outside it may seem that in today's critical debate, too, there is just a set of old ideas concerning the originality of Russia's path being bandied about, and that their anti-historical nature (i.e unwillingness to take into account twentieth-century realities) in itself condemns them to emptiness and futility.

But this is not the case. Today the 'West-East' theme is a projection of the greatest event in world history – the collapse of Soviet civilisation, the child of a totalitarian regime of unheard-of cruelty. This determines the way the 'West-East' problem is being distorted in

1

contemporary debate, its undoubted transformation into a struggle between chauvinism and its opposition.

Why do I not, in this instance, contrast the positions of Soviet and émigré commentators? The reason is that when I made a serious study of the question I discovered that in interpreting the 'West-East' theme the selfsame ideas are circulating on both sides of the frontier. Both in Soviet and in émigré criticism there are two wings or tendencies which, following Siniavskii, I would describe as 'authoritarian-nationalistic' and 'liberal-democratic':[1] in Soviet and émigré criticism alike the 'West-East' theme is today a political pseudonym for other themes, other problems. In both Soviet and émigré criticism the interpretation of 'West-East' reveals the stamp of a common mentality, formed in the conditions of a totalitarian regime and engraved with the indelible features and ways of thought of Soviet man – independent of which side of the frontier he is now on.

I suppose that all this allows me to concentrate not on comparing the treatment of the 'West-East' theme on each side of the frontier, but on the transformation of the Russo-Soviet mentality itself, on its undoubted collapse and on the processes which result from this collapse. Firstly, a model of the problem's distortion. Its internal mechanism can be revealed through the example of V. Kozhinov's article 'Hilarion's Writing and the Historical Reality of his Age'.[2] The main thing for this critic is not the writings of Hilarion, the 'Father of Russian national literature', but the elucidation of historical reality, in which the author sees a sharp opposition between the Khazar kingdom (Judaism) and Kievan Rus'. Arbitrarily interpreting the thought of the historian M. Tikhomirov, Kozhinov presents, as if taken from him, the idea that 'at the basis of the *Slovo o Zakone i Blagodati* lies the *principal* and most *acute* political and ideological problem of Old Russian life from the ninth to the early eleventh centuries: the problem of relations with and struggle against the Khazar khanate'.[3]

But having begun with 'historical reality', Kozhinov actually writes about the 'political questions' which are posed in the *Slovo o Zakone i Blagodati*. He sees in them an extremely relevant historico-philosophical conception. Kozhinov cites the words of Academician Tikhomirov: '*Under the guise of a church sermon* Hilarion in reality raised the major *political* questions *of his time*, linked with the relations between Kievan Rus' and the remains of the Khazar khanate and the Byzantine empire.'[4]

This is how Kozhinov himself proceeds, 'under the cover' of a historico-literary article propagandising a historiosophical conception in tune with the ideas of the Pamiat' movement. Deliberately distorting facts, he affirms that the Khazar yoke was 'without doubt far more dangerous for Rus' than the Tatar-Mongol yoke, particularly because Rus' was just *in the process of formation* as a people, state and culture'.[5]

It is precisely to this point that the historians of Ancient Rus', M. Robinson and L. Sazonova, have drawn attention. Exposing Kozhinov's historical falsification, they demonstrate the unscholarly nature of his ideas about the age-old struggle between Russia and Khazaria, his twisting of the facts.[6] The 'Khazar yoke' is no more than a synonym for anti-Semitism, as is the 'russophobia' which I. Shafarevich openly declares to be the cause of all Russia's ills.

Pursuing this 'model', it is impossible not to ask the following questions: (1) How could it come about that today fairly broad circles of Russians are coming together under the banner of primitive chauvinism? (2) How could it come about that the manufacturing of 'russophobia' is now the work of intellectuals, in whose ranks until recently society numbered both Kozhinov and Shafarevich, and of other experts in 'russophobia', in particular the writers V. Rasputin and V. Belov?[7] In order to understand this phenomenon, it would seem important to begin by determining the specific features of the present historical moment.

In certain Soviet and foreign journals 'perestroika' is often called a 'revolution'. In my opinion, however, it would be more accurate to say that what we are witnessing is a different type of historical moment – the *disintegration* of a Soviet civilisation that has outlived itself. It is not simply a break between different epochs, but precisely a disintegration. And, like any disintegration, it is accompanied by aggression, bitterness, outbreaks of violence, the alienation of individuals from each other within society – and even the alienation of many people, especially young people, from their country.

In an age of disintegration people do not see what awaits them. But they remember – and remember clearly – what has been and what they do *not* want. That is why in the Soviet world today everything connected with negation is growing at such a great pace.

These are the semiotics of the age.

But if today there is being born in filth, blood and torments a new civilisation, for the time being it is still fairly primitive.

As always happens at times of disintegration, the past holds people firmly in its net. Their attention is concentrated on the question of whether the October Revolution was inevitable, inherited, predetermined. At the same time there arises as an alternative in people's consciousness the question of whether the experience of freedom-loving Western countries had proved ruinous, with its diet of revolutionary ideas. 'We cannot get away from our past', writes (the possibly pseudonymous) E.N. Bich in *Daugava*, 'We are made sick by it, it holds us in its deadly grip. "Why? Where? When?", we enquire, and until we answer these questions we have no hope of moving forward.'[8]

It is true. The consciousness of many people simply cannot cope with the fact that their faith has been betrayed. As A. Shindel' writes:

> faced with the simple trap (one of a countless number!) that Stalin created, the intelligence of Soviet man falls dumb. For when Soviet man begins to understand that his holy faith has been the very roller by which he himself was crushed, then his reason simply switches off. This is his retribution for blindness.[9]

But why does reason . . . switch off?

The totalitarian regime began its triumphal march with the destruction of language (the shortest way to the destruction of a man's consciousness). As early as the mid-1920s there arose the type, brilliantly captured by Zoshchenko, of the 'ordinary' (*srednii*) man – ignorant but aggressively asserting himself as a 'leader' in the society of triumphant revolution. In the consciousness of his characters the writer immortalised what has become Soviet reality: the fictitiousness of 'personal' (*lichnostnyi*) consciousness. The proud ambition of the 'ordinary man' has supplanted 'personality'. In fact there took place what one of the heroes of Platonov's *Kotlovan* said of himself: instead of hearing his soul, he heard the noise of consciousness pouring from a loudspeaker. People began to speak in ready-made phrases and clichés which not only did not illuminate their thoughts but *ensnared* them. For the language of clichés and slogans is a 'ready-made' form, and not what Bakhtin called a pre-found word (prior discourse [*prednakhodimoe slovo*]) for a nascent idea. The clogging of the language with clichés delayed the process of assimilating reality, because people used concepts that had been quickly 'brought into use' and 'worn-out', concepts 'borrowed from outside, but not fully grasped *from within*. They had no support in the internal development of the people who used them'.[10]

Frequently what existed in the language did not exist in reality:

with this 'language', as M. Mamardashvili says, 'we "accelerated" reality itself. Precisely with its help people took account of what was going on, and frequently what happened was something of an entirely different nature from this language'.[11] And gradually the mass of people created a surreal world and learnt how to live in it. And a terrible thing happened: 'The [state's] subjects really missed out some stages in their intellectual and spiritual development . . .'.[12]

A vague consciousness, having lost its orientation in the world of causes and effects, today bears the stamp of all the chimeras that Soviet ideology has been able to produce.

Contemporary chauvinism has become one such chimera.

It has been observed that in periods of the disintegration of social order, offended national feeling functions in a variety of ways: it can lead to the 'glorification of the country's national cultural past', but it can also be directed towards a messianic vision of its civic future; often it comes out as 'the idea of revealing the decline and sins of a more developed civilization by comparison with the "virginal" national soil and so on'.[13] These 'compensational forms may also combine and appear simultaneously'.[14]

It is just such a compensational complex that lies at the basis of contemporary Russian nationalism. 'Suffering over national issues', exclaims Lichutin, 'is the instinctive, natural wish to survive in future memory.'[15] But the reality is that in a regime with a superiority complex many Soviet people are inseparable from this attitude. The last support of these lost people remains the 'imperial consciousness' nurtured by a deeply ingrained conviction that the least Soviet person, as Stalin used to say, is a whole head higher than any capitalist bureaucrat.

In a situation of being cut off from reality, deprived of the culture of abstract thinking, writes M. Mamardashvili, 'the most elementary human feeling and suffering receive a charge of negative, harmful energy . . .'.[16]

It is precisely this charge, this harmful injection that the 'national' idea has received in recent years.

But why then did there appear as ideologists of this confused consciousness, writers, artists, critics, yesterday's sowers of the sensible, the good, the eternal? Nowadays it is precisely they who appeal for a return to the 'soil', they who curse the West, considering it the source of infection, they who are the bearers of the 'Russian idea' in its debased, vulgar variant.

If Solzhenitsyn's *Odin den' Ivana Denisovicha* was an attempt to restore proud national self-awareness (as were Belov's *Privychnoe delo* or Rasputin's *Den'gi dlia Marii* and other works), then already by 1980 Belov's *Lad*, with its national ethnographic feeling, contained the juxtaposition of the 'virginal' national soil of Russia with the declining civilisation of the West; Solzhenitsyn's *Krasnoe koleso* reduces this idea to the level of historiosophy.

What are we to make of this?

I am in agreement with A. Ianov who considers that concrete historical circumstances influenced the rebirth of 'native soil' ideas: firstly, Khrushchev's denunciation of the totalitarian nature of the Stalin regime at the Twentieth Party Congress; and secondly, the crushing of the Khrushchev reform, which brought the realisation that 'revival from above' was impossible, and the crushing of the Hungarian uprising (which, it is true, I would have treated rather differently – as confirmation of the fact that the Soviet system remains an imperial, totalitarian system).[17]

But on one point I find myself in total disagreement with Ianov: it was not acquaintance with the books of Berdiaev and his 'Russian idea', as he thinks, that led to the birth of 'native soil' ideas: they ripened in Soviet reality itself and reflect the relations of Soviet man to this reality.

World War II laid bare the fundamental bases of existence and revealed that age-old national traditions were an essential component in the popular movement for victory. The state, having already in 1917 broken with national traditions, realised that without them it could not win the war. These were years when the rebirth of national feeling came from both above and below.

But these were years – especially from 1944 (when for the first time Soviet soldiers found themselves fighting beyond the frontiers of the USSR) when there flourished both state nationalism and 'imperial consciousness'.

At first state nationalism and the growing national feeling moved in the same direction. *The state exploited the national feeling* of people who were fighting for their fatherland. For this reason it turned a blind eye to the national colouring of themes and problems raised by literature in the 1960s.

But already by the end of the war national ideas 'from above' and 'from below' had diverged sharply. In semi-official ideology there was a sharp increase in the appeal to man's 'imperial' ambition. However, in its real existence the Russian people was once again cast into an abyss of poverty and humiliation.

In the role of ideologists for their people came those writers at the turn of the 1950s and 1960s who are for convenience called representatives of 'village' prose, and who have now become ideologists of chauvinism: Rasputin, Belov and others.

The writers of 'village' prose were witnesses of, or participants in, collectivisation, the famine and the war, with its defeats and victories. They had seen the people both humiliated and at the heights of heroism. Hoping that the war had brought an end to humiliation, they were deceived and bore this deception badly. In the first works of Solzhenitsyn, Rasputin, Belov and Astaf'ev were embodied a feeling of guilt towards the undervalued past, attention to popular (*narodnye*) types, and interest in the roots and sources of the people's and the nation's life (*narodno-natsional'naia zhizn'*). In the zeal with which tradition was affirmed could be seen a desire to strengthen a feeling of unshakeability, stability, confidence in the world. All this was supposed to resist the destabilisation of social and moral life which had begun in 1917. However, the main thing for the 'village writers' was the modelling of a different, 'ideal', reality, another system of ethical values based not on destructive class values but on universal human values. Their 'ideal' reality they found in the past; turning to history became a form of opposition in relation to the present. In contrast to perverted human nature was set a truth-seeker (*pravednik*). Against an inhuman regime was set the ideal peasant spiritual life of the past. Against contemporary Russia was set the image of a Russia which had in the past been great but which someone had mutilated.

And only one thing could give cause for alarm: the rejection of the regime was conducted by contrastive thinking (*myshlenie 'ot protivnogo'*). Attitudes to history and the present-day have been built on negation; positive aspirations and ideas have been amorphous and ahistorical. This zeal for negating the present-day also brings the 'village writers' close to contemporary mass consciousness.

In their way of thinking, which is inclined to operate with emasculated make-believe concepts, subjecting to the latter their studies of the contemporary world, many 'native-soil' writers share the point of view of the *'ordinary' man* (*srednii chelovek*) (understood as the leading type, formed in the bowels of the 'new historical community'). They share the same mentality. It is easy and convenient for them to talk with him and in the language of his ideas. In this way there has arisen a phenomenon first noticed by I. Rodnianskaia in a review of *Pechal'nyi detektiv*, where she wrote:

In Astaf'ev's novel 'longing for an ideal' is confused with 'longing for order' (*toska po poriadku*) and they are not one and the same thing. The writer reflected a dissatisfaction with 'customs' (*nedovol'stvo poriadkami*), characteristics of 'the man in the street', the 'man without privileges', reproducing many of the latter's swift and not always accurate social reactions.[18]

The 'social reaction' of the 'ordinary man' who, because of his surreal consciousness, cannot grasp the sources of the Russian tragedy also provide nourishment for contemporary anti-Westernisers.

This psychology, based on negation, is becoming ever more deformed. Indeed, it cannot help becoming deformed because the 'village writers' are continuing to live in a surreal world.

'I can understand Viktor Astaf'ev's anger as a human', says Merab Mamardashvili, 'I see that he is going round and round his own genuine feelings as an honest and sensitive person – but somehow he can't unravel them and understand their real origin.'[19]

Russian writers like Rasputin and Astaf'ev, writes Mamardashvili in his article, are vainly trying to revive life, 'fighting against all foreign or modernist "fancies" and invoking the traditional spirituality of the people's life and thought'. But, it must be said, behind all these words lies the same tricky distancing of reality. And, I genuinely do not understand, and would like to ask these people personally: the basic pain is the same for the Russians as for other people, perhaps even stronger, and I understand and sympathise with it completely: but do they really not detect in these moralising appeals, in this compulsory and high-flown awareness the song of the 'Mongol' and the 'Cosmic' invaders? How can their intellectual and moral senses not catch this? After all, it was with just such language and through it that all the destructive processes entered morality, spirituality, ecological harmony, and there is no need to blame industry here, for there is not any industry, no state power, no reality. It is characteristic of Russia that it has all the disadvantages and none of the advantages of contemporary phenomena. It has suffered all the harmful consequences and inadequacies of industrialisation, without having the industrialisation itself (if one does not count simply big factories with large, mainly useless, production [*bol'shie zavody, daiushchie bol'shoi val*]). In Russia there is no largescale industrial plant in the European sense. There are all the negative consequences of urbanisation, but there is no city, no phenomenon of '*urbis*'.[20]

At the present time the native-soil nationalists have merged with the old regime in one essential: the galvanisation of the basic concept of Soviet ideology – that of the 'enemy of the people'. And I agree with Siniavskii that nowadays the word 'russophobia' is a variant of the concept of 'enemy of the people'.[21] In the articles of Shafarevich, Kozhinov and others, russophobia is coming to be treated as the main reason for the ruin of Russia in 1917. Its origins are perceived as Western. Nowadays Astaf'ev, Rasputin, Belov, Maksimov and Solzhenitsyn write in the same spirit.

How are westernisers presented in the works of the russophiles? 'Like pernickety government inspectors', writes V. Lichutin, 'zealously digging up historical legends for their fairytales about our land.' They 'burrow frenziedly and without respite, supposedly from a love of truth, burrow in our history, mixing our native soil in a pile more vigorously than wild boars in the forest'.[22]

But let us allow the 'westernisers' themselves to speak, in the interests of free discussion.

The 'westernisers' are distinguished by their attempts at social analysis. 'By Russia I mean', said M. Mamardashvili, as nowadays cultural workers consider it necessary to emphasise, not 'an ethnic phenomenon but a strictly defined socio-political, domestic and socio-cultural complex, named "Russia" and uniting the most varied ethnic groups.'[23] None of these 'westernisers' defames Russia, but they try to understand man's *deformation* in the Stalin period, to rid our ideas about man of their hermetically ahistorical, atemporal nature. They proceed from an analysis of real history.

The disposition of the 'westernisers' and the 'native-soil writers' emerged very clearly in a discussion between the writer Boris Vasil'ev who made a public call to 'love Russia (even) in bad weather', and E.N. Bich in the article 'Well, What Is "Bad Weather"? An Open Letter to Boris Vasil'ev' (see note 8).

Bich refers to Chaadaev, considering that what we need today is 'a sober and merciless look at ourselves and our history'. Nor does he conceal the target of his polemic: 'And there is no point in gazing admiringly at Russia in a time of such bad weather. We have no-one to blame for it but ourselves. We ourselves are to blame for it',[24] – we and not someone from outside, not an external force like, for example, that of the 'Jews and Masons' (*zhidomasonstvo*).

But accusations of dreaming, of anti-historical thinking do not concern the russophiles of today. They are not even trying to achieve scholarly accuracy. For them scholarship is the handmaid of politics.

Recalling the scholarly aspect of the 'West-East' theme, N. Rykova, a participant in a debate on the 'Russian idea' in the journal *Iskusstvo kino*, wrote:

> It is time to understand that the question of contradictions between Russian and Western culture is nowadays artificial and inept – it does not exist. There exist in the world various historically formed cultural regions: the Western (that is, Mediterranean-European) arose organically from the ancient cultures of the Near East and Classical antiquity; there also exist Islamic and Arabic, Indian and Oriental cultures. Russian culture (even in the pre-petrine period) is not an independent unit; it belongs to the first, western one, and is as independent in it as, for example, English, German, Italian or Spanish culture. Russian culture is a whole spiritual entity (*lichnost'*) in a group of other similar entities. But these others have no common features such as would set them together in contrast to Russian culture. We are a constituent part of one great cultural region.[25]

I share the view of those who consider that the Soviet disease has always hidden its face behind borrowed masks – from Russian history or West European philosophy. In fact we have before us a completely *original* phenomenon which has never before existed either in Russia or in the West; but it cleverly exploits the 'imperial consciousness' which traces its roots to Russia's distant history. To those who are fanning the flames of hatred and enmity I say, in the words of those who think as I do, 'Be thrice accursed any rhetoric of "blood and soil". We have seen what was produced by the transformation of this rhetoric into political doctrine in Nazi Germany. Let us be watchful, let us be on our guard.'[26]

Translated by Arnold McMillin

NOTES

1. See Andrei Siniavskii, 'Dissidentstvo kak lichnyi opyt', *Sintaksis*, XV (1985), p. 142, reprinted in *Iunost'*, 5, 1989, p. 90.
2. V. Kozhinov, 'Tvorchestvo Ilariona i istoricheskaia real'nost' ego epokhi', *Voprosy literatury*, 12, 1988, p. 132.
3. Ibid., p. 137.
4. Ibid., p. 149.
5. Ibid., p. 140.

6. M. Robinson and L. Sazonova, 'Mnimaia i real'naia istoricheskaia deistvitel'nost' epokhi sozdaniia "Slova o Zakone i Blagodati" Ilariona', *Voprosy literatury*, 12, 1988, pp. 151–75.
7. There are significantly more of them than the seventy-four writers who signed.
8. E.N. Bich, 'Tak chto takoe "nepogoda"? Otkrytoe pis'mo Borisu Vasil'evu', *Daugava*, 7, 1989, p. 66.
9. A. Shindel', 'Svidetel' (Zametki ob osobennostiakh prozy Andreia Platonova', *Znamia*, 9, 1989, p. 216.
10. Merab Mamardashvili, 'D'iavol igraet nami, kogda my ne myslim tochno . . .', *Teatr*, 3, 1989, p. 93.
11. Ibid., pp. 93–4.
12. Ibid.
13. E.B. Rashkovskii and V.G. Khoros, 'Problema "Zapad-Rossiia-Vostok" v filosofskom nasledii P.Ia. Chaadaeva', in ed. L.B. Alaev *et al.*, *Vostok-Zapad, Issledovaniia. Perevody. Publikatsii* (Moscow, 1988), p. 120.
14. Ibid.
15. V. Lichutin, 'Tsel' nezrimaia . . . Razymyshleniia o russkom: utrachenom, pozabytom i merknushchem', *Druzhba narodov*, 8, 1989, p. 245.
16. *Zaria Vostoka*, 25 June 1989.
17. Aleksandr Ianov, *Russkaia ideia i 2000-i god* (New York, 1988).
18. *Literaturnaia gazeta*, 35, 1986, p. 2.
19. Merab Mamardashvili, 'D'iavol igraet nami, kogda my ne myslim tochno . . .', *Teatr*, 3, 1983, p. 96.
20. *Zaria Vostoka*, 25 June 1989.
21. Andrei Siniavskii, 'Solzhenitsyn kak ustroitel' novogo edinomysliia', *Sintaksis*, XIV (1985), p. 18.
22. V. Lichutin, op. cit., p. 235.
23. *Zaria Vostoka*, 25 June 1989.
24. E.N. Bich, 'Tak cho takoe "nepogoda"? Otkrytoe pis'mo Borisu Vasil'evu', *Daugava*, 7, 1989, pp. 65–73.
25. '"Russkaia ideia": problemy kul'tury – problemy kinematografa', *Iskusstvo kino*, 6, 1988, p. 130.
26. Ibid.

2 The Hero in Search of an Author
Zinovii Zinik

As I shall be discussing authorial motivation in émigré prose, I should like to quote an ironic passage about Zinovii Zinik from Arnold McMillin's inaugural lecture 'The Dislocation of Russian Literature':

> London-based Zinovy Zinik's *Russofobka i fungofil* disturbs any lingering complacency we may have about our own society, where phenomena as disparate as giving to the Salvation Army at Christmas, buying rounds in pubs and tending suburban gardens are excoriated as examples of British hypocrisy.[1]

I could easily dismiss accusations of maliciously anti-British (and at the same time anti-Russian) sentiments in this novel by declaring, as is usually done in such cases, that these are not my sentiments, but the sentiments of my characters. As has been said on numerous occasions in literary history, an author is not responsible for the opinions, utterances and actions of his characters. But if the author is not responsible, then who is? Of course, parents ought to be responsible for their children. An author is not identical to the hero of his novel, but the hero is a part of the author, if not in his opinions or his physiology, as it is described, then at least for the reason that the author created his hero, that is, he selected a particular character type, a particular prototype that suited his intentions. The ideological aspects of this selection are, in my view, the central feature in the metamorphoses of the émigré novel.

Returning to the quotation from Arnold McMillin, I should like to draw attention to the two words preceding my name: London-based. London is, indeed, my permanent place of residence. What is more, I hold a British passport. But . . . at this point various 'buts' arise. I also hold an Israeli passport. And besides, my prose is written in Russian, although, it is true, I occasionally write essays in English. The words London-based are a neat formulation which avoids any complicated explanation of the duality or even tribulations (from the word *tri*) of my existence. The evasiveness of formulations in such cases comes as no surprise: in many ways the opinions of the hero depend precisely upon which passport details of his émigré existence are emphasised. And this in turn depends upon who the author feels himself to be at the moment of choosing a hero for his story. And in this sense the metamorphoses of recent years have been astonishing.

Yet the main authorial dilemma remains as before. No matter who an author from Russia might consider himself to be, no matter what passport he might carry in his pocket, in his heart he does not want to part with the title of Russian writer. I wish to retain my martyr's status in belonging to Russian literature, without at the same time losing the privileges and liberties of a subject of the British crown. Even the apparently absurd extreme of such a dilemma can be pictured quite easily, when someone has completely and irrevocably gone over to the English language, yet continues to consider himself a Russian writer. (Examples of this are not difficult to find – Vladimir Nabokov, for example.) This authorial duality plays a direct role in the formation of the world-view of the hero that the author creates. To put it plainly, the more firmly the author attaches himself to Moscow (attaches in the broadest sense of the word), the more estranged becomes his description of émigré life beyond Moscow.

To write in Russian in England means to describe in Russian words things which exist only in English. For example, what is meant in Russian by *sosiska* is not a sausage at all, but rather a frankfurter. One can, of course, call an English sausage simply *angliiskaia sosiska*, as all foreigners do when they describe an English sausage. Or one can start to explain its ingredients, by telling the Russian reader, for example, that this sausage tastes like six-kopeck beefburgers, only without the coating of breadcrumbs, from the foodshops of the 1970s (for those who remember the range of products available in foodshops in the 1970s). In short, one is obliged to call things not by their proper names, but to resort to secondary associations, allusions and reminiscences from another culture. This description of a different culture by, so to speak, secondary sexual features is inevitably parodic. Precisely for this reason the aforementioned difficulties in describing a different culture are not simply a question of translation from one language to another. Rather the question of translation is 'translated' into a broader metaphysical context.

Every attempt to construct a new phrase is an attempt to clamber out of a sense of alienation, depressing in its mundaneness, into an unknown intimacy. Literature is an escape from words thrust upon you as supposedly your own (and that is what routine and mundaneness mean) into words that are foreign and unfamiliar, but which you recognise as kindred. In this sense literature is the defeat of alienation. Emigration, a final departure for foreign lands, is just one of the forms of a similar defeat of mundaneness and alienation. For this reason emigration, as a major step in life, creates the illusion of a ready-made novel. Hence such human despair when the novel does not work out, hence such authorial panic when life does not work out, far away from familiar places.

It is in our nature to meet what is alien and incomprehensible to us either with aggressive hostility or with disregard; that is, ultimately, by abandoning this alienation for hearth and home. An émigré has no choice, and if he is not an utter fool, then he will conceal his original feelings towards the alien novelty around him. Otherwise he will soon die, if not of hunger, then of depression (self-isolation). There remains, then, another sort of émigré weapon – laughter, irony, mockery. It is well known that we laugh not only in a pleasant response to paradoxical or anecdotal aspects of life, but also to hide our embarrassment and confusion. This is also disparaging laughter: we belittle in our own eyes our new environment which is threateningly mysterious and alien, tame it with satirical sketches, slap it on the back with an ironic compliment – and now we are already on a par with it. Now we can distort and disfigure names, mutilate and trample over literary quotations, modify religious doctrines and scrawl on foreign geography with the chalk of our petty consciousness.

The noble author, however, is not himself prepared to commit such a rape of foreign culture. For this reason he assigns the task of establishing firm cultural links with foreign parts to his characters. Such a character must without fail be negative. I do not know of a single positive hero in émigré literature. Still, I had better not generalise, and will rather say that there is not a single positive character in my own prose. An émigré is in himself a negative character. An émigré is a person who has rejected his motherland, has settled temporarily in a foreign country and refuses to accept his new place of residence as his present and future home. An émigré is someone who has left his motherland yet dreams of returning, if not today then tomorrow, if not tomorrow then the day after. In this sense I am not an émigré. With my dual Israeli-British citizenship I have quite enough homes, both present and future. But only comparatively recently did I realise that I pretend to be an émigré for literary reasons. More precisely, as soon as Russian literature and my 'place in it', as literary historians say, is being discussed, I automatically become an émigré.

I emigrated at a time when circles in Moscow lived according to the categories of a world, a Soviet world, divided into us and them, into good and evil. We left in order to be beyond evil, beyond the Iron Curtain. Good was identified with the views and positions of one's own circle, one's own friends, 'us'. And when I wrote about life here I naturally adapted myself to suit my reader, engaged in the 'translation' of reality here into their language. This is the 'émigré essence' of the hero. For the translation to be comprehensible it is vital to look at life abroad through the eyes of the person for whom the translation is made. Thus there emerges the character who, if not hostile, is in any event ironic in his attitude towards the reality here, which is 'alien' to our Moscow 'us'. Russian literature here stemmed precisely from the estranged, romantically isolated outlook of the outcast upon his environment. Because at his back stood people for whom this outlook was 'their own'. But with the collapse of the Iron Curtain, we are all beyond good and evil (in the Soviet understanding of this division – into those who are for the regime and dissidents). Circles of friends have turned into circles on murky water. Friends have remained friends, but have ceased to be a circle. And the vision of my hero, undivided in its animosity, has also disintegrated. He no longer looks back with a nostalgic smile at his Moscow past, for it has been transformed into a handful of scattered partners in conversation, lacking the inspiration of separation.

There is no longer any division into literature of the emigration and literature of the metropolis – or so it would seem. Yet the two have not merged into one. Previously, émigré status bore a political label too, it was shackled to the Iron Curtain, it was of a moralistic, didactic nature. The Curtain fell, the dungeons crumbled and we were straight away appended to Moscow. Colonisation took place, the centralisation of literature; the émigré is transformed from an isolated outcast into a vassal of the literary metropolis. Of course I have rid myself of my émigré status in life, but Russian literature, not to mention Russian culture, is not so liberal. In Russian literary history one's division into an Englishman (a Jew, a Tatar, a Balt) in life and a Russian 'in words alone' is not possible. In literature I remain an émigré. I remain a foreigner. From an external émigré in respect of Russian literature I am transformed into an internal émigré.

Everything returns to its starting-point: this was where I began, from internal emigration. I fled from Soviet literature but now I am once more appended to it. Having become an internal émigré with regard to Russian literature only here (that is, having ceased to look back at my Russian literary environment), I am beginning to rid myself of my parodic (that is, seen through a Russian's eyes) perception of English *realia*. That is, I am ceasing to translate (that is, to parody). That is, I see and hear like some Englishman of a rather strange and monstrous kind – thinking in English but expressing himself in Russian. But is not this, then, the end of Russian literature? Or is Russian literature in, so to speak, 'Russian' English a possibility – that is the question.

As a person I have felt less and less desire in recent years to leave London, this island, even to go to Paris. I love Newcastle Brown Ale and The Famous Grouse whisky, I adore fish-and-chips, misty lawns and country pubs, Sunday papers and the cliffs of Dover, Shakespeare and the Queen. I do not intend to move back to Moscow. But not without cause do I switch to English when enumerating the things I love in Albion – not only because I am too lazy to translate specifically English aspects of daily life and existence here into another language, but also because the acceptance of a reality, until recently alien, is in practice impossible in a foreign, in relation to that reality, language. When discussion turns to Russian literature, the entire astonishing list of personal discoveries disappears before one's very eyes like invisible ink. The question is: whether it is possible to translate into your native language something that enchants you precisely because it seems impossible to translate into another language? Can something that is not ours become kindred? How is it possible verbally to realise, accept and understand what is foreign, if foreignness means precisely that which it is impossible to realise, accept and understand?

Translated by Galya and Hugh Aplin

NOTE

1. Arnold B. McMillin, *Changing Places: The Dislocation of Russian Literature* (London, 1989) p. 10.

3 England in Russian Émigré Poetry: Iosif Brodskii's 'V Anglii'

Gerald Stanton Smith

V Londone tozhe ne polezhish'

Lev Loseff

As we all know, the literary capital of the First Wave of Russian émigrés, at least after 1925 when economic circumstances made Berlin lose its advantages, was Paris; there were outlying centres in the Slavonic capitals of Prague, Sofia, and Warsaw; there was an even more peripheral outpost in Harbin. After World War II, the centre of gravity shifted to the USA. The Third Wave of emigration has had a triple centre: Paris, the home since 1974 of its most important journal, *Kontinent*; New York, the place of publication and residence of a large number of its writers; and, in contrast to the earlier situation, Israel. During the entire seventy-year history of the Russian literary emigration, the British Isles has been marginal territory, for various reasons which – while not too controversial – are too complicated to go into in the present essay.[1]

In these circumstances, it is fairly easy to make a brief survey of the poetry that has been composed in and about England by Russian émigré authors since 1917.[2] The story begins with what remains the most substantial body of such poetry, composed by Vladimir Nabokov during his time as an undergraduate at the University of Cambridge from 1919 to 1921. Nabokov thought of himself as a Russian poet at this time;[3] his output in England consists of a number of lyrics, most of them nostalgic and retrospective, dealing with his lost Russia rather than his new place of residence. But there are several interesting poems that deal with Nabokov's experience as an undergraduate and with his visits to various parts of England.[4] The single most important work is the long *Universitetskaia poema* of 1927.[5] Among other fascinating aspects of this work is the passage describing the football match with the hero in goal, an interesting intertext

17

with the precisely contemporaneous match in Olesha's short novel *Zavist'*, the British amateur ethos of Nabokov's game standing at the opposite pole from the professional and international element in Olesha's.

After Nabokov left England, it was ten years before another Russian poet made a significant contribution while based in England. But there were some birds of passage, including two very big ones. One was Khodasevich, who came through England on his way to Ireland in 1923 and apparently said nothing whatsoever about it, except simply to report the fact in his letters.[6] The other was Marina Tsvetaeva, who came to London for two weeks in 1926 at the invitation of D.S. Mirskii. Again, she reported on the visit in her letters, notably in one to Pasternak whose lyrical prose approaches the force of her poetry,[7] but she did not apparently write any actual verse during her visit.

By the time he invited Tsvetaeva to England – he spent the years 1922–32 teaching at the School of Slavonic Studies[8] – D.S. Mirskii had long since given up the idea of being a poet. His first book, published in 1911 when he was twenty-one, had been a collection of lyrics. While he was in England, though, Mirskii did translate some poetry into Russian from English. This was part of a literary game. Maurice Baring, Mirskii's friend and sponsor, was among many other things a reputable English poet, and in the mid-1920s he had the idea of getting a number of his foreign friends to translate some of his poems into their native languages, and published the results together, as if the English originals were in fact·the translations. Mirskii was chosen to provide Russian 'originals' for two of the poems, and he did so with considerable wit.[9]

The next person to write Russian poetry in England was connected with both Nabokov and Mirskii. Gleb Struve was Nabokov's friend in the early 1920s; he was at Oxford while Nabokov was at Cambridge, and the two knew each other very well in Berlin after 1921. In 1932 Struve replaced Mirskii at the School of Slavonic Studies. He stayed until 1946, when he went to Berkeley in one of the many moves referred to earlier as articulating the shift in the centre of gravity of the emigration from Europe to North America. Struve is rightly most famous as the author of the only history we have so far of any phase of Russian literature in emigration. He was also, though, a poet, if only a minor one. Among his lyrics are some that were written during his time in England; in fact, one of them would appear to be the only contemporaneous poem in Russian besides Akhmatova's famous lyric to deal with the London Blitz.[10]

There is one more Russian poet who deserves mention in this context. This is Ekaterina Bakunina, who was the editorial secretary of the Paris periodical *Chisla*, and whose poetry was published in the inter-war period in *Sovremennye zapiski* and other journals of the emigration. Bakunina apparently came to live in England in the mid-1930s, but it has proved impossible to discover what became of her.[11] The Pasternak family moved to Oxford just before World War II, and several interesting poems have been written by the sisters about their new home.[12] Of the other émigrés of the first wave, Iurii Ivask visited England in the late 1960s and wrote one exquisite lyric about a country churchyard in Rutland.[13] Georgii Adamovich was at one time visiting lecturer at the University of Manchester, but the experience bore no fruit in terms of poetry.

The poets of the Second Wave of émigrés avoided Britain altogether. There were no employment opportunities here that compared with those in the USA. And alas, when the Third Wave of emigration started to arrive in the early 1970s, the situation was similar: the universities started their retrenchment at exactly this time. But a small number of poets have settled here. Evgenii Dubnov has been resident in England and publishing poetry and translations with some success since he moved from Israel. Igor' Pomerantsev is a very welcome presence at this conference. Apart from these residents, a few poets have passed through and left one or two impressions. Iurii Kublanovskii looks back into the Tudor period in one set of poems.[14] And Lev Druskin has published a batch of poems, some of them dealing with Scotland;[15] they are very good examples of what might be called tourist poetry, with some very familiar themes: the persistent presence of history, the peculiar people, the unpredictable weather.

Among all these scraps and fragments, Iosif Brodskii's sequence 'V Anglii' stands out in many ways. To begin with, it is easily the most substantial piece of poetry devoted to England on the basis of first-hand experience by a Russian poet of any period. It was first published in *Kontinent* in 1977, and collected in *Uraniia* (Ann Arbor, 1987), where it occupies pp. 74–80. A translation of it in the author's English made jointly with one of its dedicatees, Alan Myers, appears in Brodskii's *A Part of Speech* (Oxford, 1980, pp. 126–7). The sequence consists of seven numbered segments; they are of twenty-two, twenty, twenty-six, fifty-four, twenty-four, fifty-six, and twelve lines, a total of 214 lines, which is the size of a modest *poema*; it exemplifies that thrust towards major form that is a constant element in Brodskii's poetics. There is insufficient space here to offer anything like a thoroughgoing analysis of the sequence in its entirety; instead, a few general remarks will be made, followed by a more detailed look at one segment of the sequence, the penultimate and longest, 'York'.

Five of the seven segments have place-names as titles: they move from south to north, beginning on the south coast with Brighton; the next three parts are located in London (North Kensington, Soho, East Finchley); then comes the fifth segment, 'Three Knights', which is set in an abbey church whose location is not specified. The sixth section, as already mentioned, is entitled 'York'. The last piece has no title, but seems to be set in York again, or thereabouts. In this spread of locations for the poems of 'V Anglii' we see evidence of Brodskii's studied individualism, for the places he chooses are, with the exception perhaps of Soho, unconventional and atypical for foreigners looking at the country. It is *North* Kensington instead of the much more familiar *South* Kensington; the unremarkable northern suburb of East Finchley. The choice of locations gives the impression that we are hearing from someone who has penetrated into the fastnesses of ordinary English life rather than being in the country as a tourist and looking at the famous places. This is the first and most salient feature about Brodskii's England compared with those of other Russian poets who have dealt with the subject.

There are several elements that the various parts of Brodskii's England have in common. The most surprising one is the absence of people. We meet some anonymous drinkers in Soho, a suburban gardener and his second wife in Finchley, and a shabby man seeing his daughter off on the train in the last poem of the sequence. But in general, Brodskii's England is empty of human beings. There are two cases of other people speaking during the course of 'V Anglii', but they are broken-off fragments of statements and do not involve any interplay between the author and the character concerned. In this respect, Brodskii's England resembles the other settings that occur in his poetry; he creates a world populated principally by the cold eye and intellect of the first-person observer, who communicates with himself in monologue and soliloquy.

Another principal feature of Brodskii's England that is character-istic of his settings anywhere in the world is the absence of colour. It is true that many flowers and trees are named in the course of the sequence, and their colours thereby implied, but as a rule colours are not actually named; they are left to the imagination. One suspects that the phonetic value of Brodskii's terminology is perhaps the most important motivating factor in his choice of objects to name.

It should go without saying that the various segments of the England sequence are unified by the now very familiar Brodskii tone: dispassionate, intellectual, with an absence of emotional reference and an abundance of ratiocination. Characteristically, the poems proceed as an alternation between observation (which is usually a matter of listing rather than description with evaluation) and abstract meditation. Very often, these meditations are concerned with measuring things (commonly, phenomena belonging to different orders) against each other and forming hierarchies. A characteristic case occurs near the end of 'York', where man is said to be less than Time. Again, as is usual in Brodskii, there is a general preoccupation with the nature of Time and Space in relation to human existence.[16]

Let us now turn specifically to 'York'. This segment may be seen to contain the central core of the work as a whole; in it, Brodskii essays a definition of what England is. 'York' is also the most personal of the seven constituent poems of the sequence. In part, it is an elegy for W.H. Auden, who has received the most profound tribute Brodskii has ever addressed to another poet – it may be the most profound tribute ever from a Russian poet to an Anglophone poet – the essay 'To Please a Shadow', in which Brodskii declares that everything he has ever written is addressed to Auden.[17] We find embedded in the text of 'York' a statement by Auden that can only be fully understood with the aid of this essay, where its authorship and context are specified ('I have known three great poets . . .'). Auden was born in York. The most powerful element in Brodskii's poem that recalls Auden is that same formal property that Brodskii seems to have assimilated from him early on: the sinuous movement of the poem through time and space in a series of extended, complex, form-breaching meditative statements.

The most surprising and original element in the accessories of the York poem is that Brodskii has chosen what most people would consider an untypical state of the weather. It is almost mandatory for foreign poets writing about England to speak of fog, mist, rain, gloom, clouds. Brodskii, however, has his visit to York take place on a day that is bristling with heat. It is high summer, with plentiful butterflies (the most persistent single image in the poem), willow herb, and burdock; there is no wind, a cloudless sky, and a relentless sun.

We should not be surprised, though, knowing Brodskii's usual ways of proceeding, when halfway through the poem (lines 43–4) the setting turns into a vacuum. By the time we have got this far into the text, we appreciate that the title of the poem is somewhat misleading. Despite the streets with tiled roofs, the setting is not York the tourist city, with its unavoidable Minster, Castle, Jorvik and Railway Museums, but rather the county of Yorkshire. The landscape that becomes a vacuum is in fact a rural one, despite the very Audenesque 'dead factory' that we have met in line 2.

As always in Brodskii, the topographical specificity of the poem's title belies the presence in the text of themes and ideas that are not localised. It was mentioned earlier that the poem is an elegy for Auden. The elegy is one of the most frequently encountered genres in Brodskii's poetry, and he has said several interesting things about this genre in his essays. The gist of these statements is that no matter to whom an elegy is addressed, whoever it is that has died and is being commemorated and celebrated, the elegy is always a poem about the poet's own self. And so it turns out here. Auden, and after him Chester Kallman, have disappeared, never to return, by the time we get to line 13 of this 56-line text (unless Auden stands behind the *tebia* of line 43, which seems doubtful). The poem then becomes a first-person meditation on Time and human purpose. The most personal section of it, which occupies the fifth stanza, laments the poet's failing powers and registers his increasing sense of desolation.

The stanza that stands formally at the centre of the poem, the fourth, is where the local theme is brought to a head. Here we find a definition of England, in a baffling example of Brodskii's insouciant seeming-sequiturs. England, we are told, is a place where the world flows into (*slivaetsia v*) a long street where other people live. We are pleased to learn that 'therefore' in this sense Brodskii considers that England is still an empire and capable of ruling the waves. This latter capacity also arises as a result of England's 'water-burbling' music. The imperial theme returns in the last stanza with a vision of one of the Roman roads running north from York, dwarfed by the willow herb, and forgotten by Rome itself.

The local element, though, has long since been negated by Brodskii. Line 20 presents a general statement that defines and at the same time justifies Brodskii's topographical poetry: 'Man brings with him his dead end (*tupik*) into any point in the world'. This idea of being in a state of captivity is picked up at the end of the poem, but obliquely: the last stanza states the familiar and perhaps central Brodskii notion that man's word endures in Time much more successfully than does his body. Here we have an appropriate conclusion for a poem that started out as an elegy for another poet.

The movement of the argument in 'York', as so often in Brodskii, is from somewhere to nowhere, from something to nothing, from the concrete to the abstract, from particular location in Time and Space (summer, York) to the infinite (vacuum, the sky). In poems such as 'York', the England sequence, and his topographical poems in general, Brodskii has created what is now geographically the widest-ranging body of work in the history of Russian poetry. But in this poem, as everywhere in Brodskii, we soon find that the specific locations all lead to the same existential, metaphysical dilemma.

NOTES

1. There is no history of the Russian emigration in England; a valuable concise account of the situation between the wars is presented in Pyotr Petrovich Shidlovsky, 'Here is Imperial Russia . . .', in Michael Glenny and Norman Stone, *The Other Russia. The Experience of Exile* (London and Boston, 1990), pp. 289-97.
2. Russian poets who spent time in England before 1917 notably include: Antiokh Kantemir, in London between 1732 and 1738; Nikolai Karamzin, who visited England in 1789; Konstantin Batiushkov, who came in 1814, and Anna Bunina, who came in 1816. Nikolai Ogarev resided in London from 1856 until the mid-1860s, when he moved to Geneva; he returned shortly before his death in 1877. Konstantin Bal'mont visited England, and in particular Oxford, in 1897; his poems about England include the cycle 'Iz Anglii', published in the collection *Tishina* (St Petersburg, 1898); three of the poems were included in Konstantin Bal'mont, *Stikhotvoreniia* (Leningrad, 1969), pp. 134–5. Samuil Marshak lived in England from 1912 to 1914, an episode which has not yet been properly researched or discussed; it was during this time that he began translating British poetry. For some of the original poetry of Marshak from this period see his *Stikhotvoreniia i poemy* (Leningrad, 1973), pp. 173–4. Kornei Chukovskii visited England with an official delegation in 1916, and returned in 1963. Nikolai Gumilev was in London in 1917. Nikolai Minskii lived in England after the Revolution, working at the Soviet Consulate in London.
3. See Vladimir Nabokov, *Drugie berega* (New York, 1954), pp. 226–30. It would be interesting to discover the identity of Nabokov's Russian fellow-student who 'called himself a Socialist, wrote unrhymed verse, and was a remarkable expert on (let's say) Egyptian history' (ibid., p. 223). The reference to poetry-writing is omitted from the corresponding passage in *Speak, Memory* (New York, 1966), p. 262.
4. For some of the poems written in Cambridge, see Vladimir Nabokov, *Stikhi* (Ann Arbor, Michigan, 1979), pp. 23-40, 48-49, 56.
5. Vladimir Nabokov, 'Universitetskaia poema', *Sovremennye zapiski*, XXXIII (1927), pp. 223–54. The poem has not so far been reprinted.
6. David Bethea, *Khodasevich: His Life and Art* (Princeton, 1983), p. 265.
7. Letters written by Tsvetaeva during her stay in London include one to

Anna Teskova (Marina Tsvetaeva, *Pis'ma k A. Teskovoi* [Prague, 1969], p. 38); and two to Prince D.A. Shakhovskoi (Marina Tsvetaeva, *Neizdannye pis'ma* [Paris, 1972], pp. 361–3); in a letter to Boris Pasternak of 1928 which clearly reflects her impressions of her visit, Tsvetaeva suggested that they meet some time in London (ibid., p. 317).

8. On Mirskii's life see most recently G.S. Smith, 'D.S. Mirsky, Literary Critic and Historian', in D.S. Mirsky, *Uncollected Writings on Russian Literature* (Oakland, 1989).

9. See Nina Lavroukine, 'Maurice Baring and D.S. Mirsky: A Literary Relationship', *The Slavonic and East European Review*, LXI, 1 (1984), pp. 25–35.

10. 'London – 1940', in Gleb Struve, *Utloe zhil'e. Izbrannye stikhi 1915-1949gg.* (Munich, 1965), p. 74; 'Londontsam', in Anna Akhmatova, *Stikhotvoreniia i poemy* (Leningrad, 1976), pp. 208–9. Other poems by Struve with English by-lines include 'Ia p'ian toboiu, ne vinom' (1941, High Barnet); 'Na reke' (1941, Oxford); 'V.F. Khodasevichu, 2' (1943, London): see *Utloe zhil'e*, pp. 75, 77–8, 82 respectively.

11. For a selection of Bakunina's poetry, see *Sodruzhestvo. Iz sovremennoi poezii russkogo zarubezh'ia* (Washington, 1966), pp. 36–43; for a brief autobiography, see ibid., p. 508. Bakunina is listed as resident in London in this publication.

12. See Zhozefina Pasternak, *Pamiati Pedro* (Paris, 1981), pp. 70, 71, 88, 89; Lidiia Pasternak Sleiter, *Vspyshki magniia* (Geneva, 1974), pp. 39–58.

13. Iurii Ivask, 'Voskresenie v Rutlande', *Novyi zhurnal*, LXXXIX (1967), pp. 87–8.

14. Iurii Kublanovskii, 'Britanskie stansy', in *Vstrechi. Al'manakh. Ezhegodnik* (Philadelphia, 1988), pp. 23–7.

15. Druskin, *Kontinent* (1984). At the time of going to press the author was unable to check this reference.

16. For discussion of various aspects of the 'V Anglii' sequence, see Valentina Polukhina, *Joseph Brodsky. A Poet for Our Time* (Cambridge, New York, Port Chester, Melbourne, Sydney, 1989), per index.

17. Joseph Brodsky, 'To Please a Shadow,' in his *Less than One* (New York, Toronto, Harmondsworth, 1980).

4 Home and Abroad in the Works of Brodskii
Lev Loseff

I

Just three years before Brodskii moved to the West a book was published in Moscow in which Iu.M. Lotman formulated his renowned narratological principle: 'An event in a text is the displacement of a character across the border of a semantic field'.[1] The subject of a lyric poet's work is his life. The fourth of June 1972, the date of his irrevocable crossing of a non-metaphorical border, is the chief event in the subject that is Brodskii's life, and he has described it with such physiological penetration that all the examples cited by the Tartu philologist pale before it:

> *Duia v poluiu dudku, chto tvoi fakir,*
> *ia proshel skvoz' stroi ianychar v zelenom,*
> *chuia iaitsami kholod ikh zlykh sekir,*
> *kak pri vkhode v vodu. I vot, s solenym*
> *vkusom etoi vody vo rtu,*
> *ia peresek chertu . . . (ChR, 100)[2]*

This was written in 1975, but the same can be found in verse composed immediately after the *event*:

> *Boiazno! To-to i est', chto boiazno.*
> *Dazhe kogda vse kolesa poezda*
> *prokatiatsia s grokhotom nizhe poiasa,*
> *ne zamiraet polet fantazii.*
> *Tochno rasseiannyi vzor otlichnika,*
> *ne otlichaia ochki ot lifchika,*
> *bol' blizoruka, i smert' rasplyvchata,*
> *kak ochertan'ia Azii. (ChR, 25)*

We should note that in the multi-layered (conceited) metaphors the evil forces, the border-guards of the Leningrad airport, are called

25

'janissaries', while death is likened to Asia. We shall return to this later, but first we should remark upon one peculiarity.

The fact is that from the very beginning in Brodskii's poetry a motif was visibly present that Tsiavlovskii called, applying it to the work of Pushkin, 'abroadsickness'. 'Never yet had I seen a foreign land. The border held something mysterious for me; since the years of my childhood travels have been my most cherished dream', wrote Pushkin.[3] Much of early Brodskii is imbued with this Pushkinian mood, for example the long poem 'Pis'mo v butylke' ('Letter in a Bottle', 1965). The difference is that in Pushkin's time the myth of an insurmountable state frontier (*'granitsa na zamke!'*) was not yet instilled into the consciousness of Russian people. Brodskii's lyric hero accepts from the start the fact of his incarceration within the Soviet state and the impenetrability of the border. In 'Pis'mo v butylke' *'vzor passazhir ustremil na Vest'* (*OVP*, 148), but the ship on which he is sailing is fatally locked in the Northern ice. Parting with guests from abroad the poet writes *'navsegda rasstaemsia'* (*OVP* 174), or else *'negde . . . do smerti nam vstrechat'sia bole (krome umozritel'nogo svidaniia v zvezdnom nebe)'* (*KPE*, 80). In the poem 'Konets prekrasnoi epokhi' ('The End of a Fine Age') he finds a remarkable expression for the geographical solipsism characteristic of many Russian intellectuals of his generation: *'kartu Evropy ukrali agenty vlastei'* (*KPE*, 59). In the same work he proposes with bitter sarcasm such fantastic escape plans (*'dernut' otsiudova po moriu novym Khristom'*) that, by comparison, Pushkin's plan to flee abroad disguised as Aleksei Vul'f's servant seems quite realistic.

Incidentally, in his early youth Brodskii was initiated by a romantically-inclined friend into his plan to hijack a Soviet aeroplane and fly abroad. Although this plan remained the whim of a youthful imagination, the powers-that-be learned of it, and it was with this episode that the poet's real difficulties with State Security began. It is characteristic that when they set about Brodskii seriously, although the formal charge and grounds for conviction was 'parasitism', in fact the central charge, in the speeches of the prosecution and in the newspaper campaign, was that of a lack of patriotism and, still worse, a love for foreign countries. His ideological persecutors persistently ascribed to the poet lines which he never wrote: *'Ia liubliu stranu chuzhuiu'*. Evidence of Brodskii's criminal antipatriotism was discerned, for example, in the fact that in a letter he addressed one of his friends not as 'comrade', but as 'sir'.[4] In the one-dimensional consciousness of Brodskii's persecutors love for foreign countries precluded love for one's own. Many years later, in the poem 'Razvivaia Platona' ('Developing Plato') Brodskii recalls quite good-naturedly the crowd which *'besnuias' vokrug krichala,/ tycha v menia natruzhennymi ukazatel'nymi: "Ne nash!"'* (*U*, 10). But even people from what might have seemed to be another camp had no doubts about Brodskii's lack of patriotism. *'Uekhal ty v dalekie predely,/ kuda davno glaza tvoi gliadeli'* – thus, after Brodskii's departure, simply but sincerely, wrote a man who in his youth had considered him a friend.

The desire to leave Russia and live in the West really was expressed by, and not just ascribed to, Brodskii. Such moods are widely represented in his works, starting with the very earliest. However, since we are talking about poetic utterances, they are comprehensible only in context. Contextually, the geographical or, if you like, the geopolitical theme in Brodskii's work was always defined by the constant opposition of 'Russia – The West', expressed paradigmatically in opposing sets of images: 'Islam – Christianity', 'The Wood – The Sea', 'Cold – Heat' and, long before it entered everyday political vocabulary, 'Stagnation – Movement'.[5] When Brodskii wrote late in 1970: *'A nynche ia okhvachen zharom!/ Mne sil'no khochetsia otsel'!'* it was not simply information in a letter to a friend about his plans for emigration, expressed just for fun in four-footed iambs and in rhyme. Both *heat* and *movement* relate these simple lines to the constant image of the *frozen* (in both senses – cold and immobility) empire:

> *I klimat tam nedvizhim, v toi strane,*
> *otkuda vse – kak son bol'noi v istome.* (*OVP*, 24)

The consistent system of imagery developed in Brodskii's poetry for the expression of the theme 'Russia – The West' can be translated with astonishing precision into the language of Eurasian philosophy, which has shown such strong signs of life recently in Soviet Russia. Compare, for example, the utterance of one of the neo-Eurasians, Dmitrii Balashov: 'The border between Russia and the West is a negative January isotherm'. As is remarked by Boris Paramonov, from whose article I have drawn this amazingly vivid aphorism, even Konstantin Leont'ev did not manage to say anything like that.[6]

Similarly Eurasian in its essence is the opposition of the images 'Islam – Christianity'. In one of the key works of Eurasianism, 'O turanskom elemente v russkoi kul'ture' ('On the Turanian Element in Russian Culture'), Nikolai Sergeevich Trubetskoi wrote that 'the chief cultural gravitation of the Turanians (and thus of the Russians, too) is towards Islam'. According to Trubetskoi, 'the Christianity of the Russians is not organic, they rework it in an Islamic fashion: the main religious characteristic of the Russians is so-called daily confessionalism, that is, the organisation of private and communal life according to a severe (quasi-ecclesiastical) canon'.[7] Although the Eurasians' works were not widely available in Brodskii's youth, his meditations on Russia and the West, stemming from the same tradition – from the Slavophiles to Dostoevskii, Vladimir Solov'ev and Blok – were similar. True – and the distinction is significant – the attitude of the poet-thinker to these *realia* was different. Esenin, unconsciously adopting Eurasian sentiments in his work, writes of the Asiatic aspects of Moscow lovingly:

> *Ia liubliu etot gorod viazovyi,*
> *Pust' obriuzg on i pust' odriakh,*
> *Zolotaia, dremotnaia Aziia*
> *Opochila na kupolakh.*[8]

In Brodskii we find:

> *polumesiats plyvet v zapylennon okonnom stekle*
> *nad krestami Moskvy, kak likhaia pobeda Islama. (KPE, 101)*

And again, '*kalendar' Moskvy zarazhen koranom*' (*KPE*, 6); and, finally, the defenders of the Soviet frontier are 'janissaries'.

In contrast to the Eurasians, who insisted on the originality of 'East-Western', that is, Eurasian, Russia, Brodskii would have preferred quite unambiguously a Russia after the Western model. In 'Pis'mo v butylke' he sadly and tenderly cites long lists of names that are symbolic of Western culture – from St Francis to Hollywood's Errol Flynn. He dedicates heartfelt elegies to such masters of Western poetry as John Donne and T.S. Eliot, who are quite alien to traditional Russian culture. But what is considerably more important, even in the first period of his work he introduces into his Russian verse form a profoundly Western poetic, not to be found in Russian poetry before him, and with it a poetic outlook on life from the European Baroque and English Modernism. Although Brodskii never wrote the incriminating line '*Ia liubliu stranu chuzhuiu*', he did nevertheless indeed love it deeply, if by the words 'foreign land' one means a sort of continent of Western culture.

And it is here that the question arises: why are the overwhelming majority of Brodskii's poems reflecting his experience in the West imbued with a sense of longing, despair, or at best, resignation? Moreover, we are not talking about a gradual disenchantment. A tragic, alienated perception of Western reality appears in literally the first things he wrote outside of Russia. Why then is the 'Westerniser' Brodskii not happy in the West?

The answer may be simple: the poet loves his homeland more than foreign countries. If Brodskii's patriotism and love for his homeland are oddly expressed, then it is precisely the oddities of this love that define Brodskii as a truly Russian poet. Here some explanation is essential.

II

We have called Brodskii a 'Westerniser'. 'Occidentophilism' and 'Slavophilism' are outdated terms which even to begin with were not entirely serious, and we are using them for want of better ones in the following sense. Westernisers are those who perceive Russian culture as a part of general European culture with its roots in Greece and Rome, as a culture formed by Christianity and – a central factor in the self-definition of a Russian Westerniser – a culture which contrasts with 'The East'. The Slavophiles, whose name is even more foolish, attempt to describe Russian culture as fundamentally distinct from that of the West and of the East. From the Slavophiles' point of view, Western religious faith and Western conceptions of man and society are inapplicable to Russian life, ruinous for Russian society and for individual Russians. From their point of view, the Westernisers consider that the features of the Russian way of life distinguished by the Slavophiles as central – 'the swarming life' celebrated by Lev Tolstoi – are extracultural phenomena, not the result of historical creation by the people, but, so to speak, the unfinished remnants of the cultural process, unsubdued chaos. Insofar as human communal life is not possible in utterly chaotic conditions, the vacuum is filled by primitive and cruel forms of 'Eastern' social organisation, which are hostile to the individual.

If in its naïve period, up until the work of the early Pushkin – 'Derevnia', 'Vol'nost'' – Russian poetry was 'Westernising' through and through, thenceforth classic Russian poetry of the nineteenth century was to a great extent coloured by Slavophilism. I have in mind not only the Slavophile poetic declarations of Khomiakov or

Tiutchev. Almost all Russian lyric verse of the nineteenth century from the late Pushkin to the Decadents is imbued with a worldview that could be called Slavophile. Russian lyric poets of the period together performed a huge cultural-historical task – they taught themselves and their readers to perceive Russia aesthetically *just as it is*. The aesthetic experience of the ordinary, unexceptional, even the negative as beautiful, defines to a significant degree the unique character and success of Russian lyric verse of the last century. The very monotonous flatness of the Russian terrain, the commonplace nature of our national wildlife (birches, rowans, daisies, cornflowers, which can be found worldwide), the fickle climate with the sky more often grey than blue, the extreme simplicity of wooden folk architecture, even the poverty of daily life become the object of patriotic love for Russian lyric poets. Lermontov in his poem 'Rodina' ('The Motherland'), known to every schoolchild, called this love 'strange'. The poet could not understand intellectually the love he felt with his soul. Love for another motherland, the arena of the heroic past, was considered not 'strange', but 'natural' (*'slava, kuplennaia krov'iu'*, *'temnoi stariny zavetnye predan'ia'*). This motherland looked quite different from the usual Russia accessible to the eye. It was packed full of mountains and crags on which for the most part there grew oak trees. In mysterious valleys between the crags rapid torrents were flowing and swans were flying. That is, in the years when Lermontov's taste was being formed it was thought natural, and not strange, to feel love for a motherland of conventions, decorated in the style of a sort of Bavaria, perhaps, in place of the genuine Russia outside the window, where you see an aspen more often than an oak, and a jackdaw or crow more often than a swan. The Russia of poetic conventions was populated with ideal citizens and yeomen quite unlike the real drunken peasants and station-masters.

In point of fact, the 'strangeness' of Lermontov's love was the guarantee of success for Russian realistic lyric verse – after all, lyric poetry is actually the art-form of internal conflict that cannot be resolved by the intellect. *'Odi et amo'*, said the writer deemed to be one of the first lyric poets in European history. *'I strast', i nenavist' k otchizne'*, repeated the writer who stands on the border between the poetic tradition of the nineteenth century and new Russian poetry. And although Catullus had a woman in mind, and not a country, Blok's utterance is equivalent to that of the Roman, for in the Symbolist's consciousness the country and a woman are fused: *'O Rus' moia, zhena moia . . .'*.

I read in a book of memoirs about the artist Ivan Shishkin, who was on one occasion working on a study of a field and a forest's edge. A peasant woman was passing by, but stopped to gaze at the canvas. 'Do you like it?', asked Shishkin. 'Very much', sighed the woman. And at this point Shishkin, the realist of all realists, whose painting is sometimes compared with photography, got it into his head to go and ask, 'What is it I'm painting?'. The woman became confused, blushed, looked closely at the canvas and said uncertainly: 'It looks like the tomb of our Lord . . .'. Just as the eye of a simple peasant woman was not trained to read the perspectives, the chiaroscuro and so on that make up the language of realistic painting, so the eye of Russian readers up to the middle of the last century was not trained to read descriptions of their native reality. They would look at aspen woods and hummocks, peasant men and women, but would see groves of oak trees, crags, yeomen. And if they could not contrive to perceive groves of oak trees, crags and yeomen, then they considered what they saw devoid of aesthetic meaning, formless, deformed.

From the verse of Lermontov, Tiutchev, Aleksei Tolstoi and Nekrasov, the real Russian landscape and the Russian way of life migrated to Russian prose, then subsequently was fixed on canvas in the painting of Savrasov, Vasil'ev and Levitan. But I want particularly to emphasise the pragmatic, all-enveloping nature of Russian lyric verse and its role in altering the Russian reader's perception of the world.

Compare two contemporaries' perceptions of such an everyday object as a *tarantas*, a carriage of simple construction in which people travelled or transported goods. This is how it is described by Vladimir Sollogub:

> Imagine two long shafts, two parallel staffs of oak, immeasurable and endless. Between them, as though tossed there by mistake, is a huge basket, rounded at the sides like a giant goblet, like a chalice from antediluvian feasts. At the ends of the oaken staffs wheels are attached, and the whole strange creation seems from a distance some weird product of the world of the fantastic, something between a dragon-fly and a hooded wagon.[10]

If an indispensable attribute of the Russian landscape, the *tarantas*, enters the field of vision of a satirist of the Romantic school, it is perceived as something inescapably ugly and the mode of description is deeply ironic. The new lyric poet looks at and sees the Russian world around him quite differently, seeing not the ugliness of individual objects, but the beauty of their harmonious interplay. Thus Fet in his memoirs looks admiringly at N.N. Tolstoi who could 'more naturally than anyone ride on this troika, in this tarantass and across this land'.[11] Of course, it is not a question of whose description is better, for they are not comparable. And they cannot be compared, not because Sollogub is a prose-writer and Fet a poet (albeit writing in this instance in prose), but because Sollogub is still a Romantic, while Fet is already a Realist. 'Russian poetry of the nineteenth century – of its first half especially – should be read if only because it gives you an idea of what gave birth to that century's Russian psychological novel', says Iosif Brodskii.[12] And when Fet, a few lines below those already cited, gives us a delightful pictorial description of two 'drunken draymen, one dark, one ginger, dancing before the entrance to a tavern, without regard for the baking sun',[13] we are dealing with a new aesthetic perception, which the reader Fet was presented with by the poet Lermontov.

It would be a serious mistake to reduce the question of the 'Occidentalism' and 'Slavophilism' of Russian poets, including modern Russian poets, to their political orientation. The very definition 'Russian poet' is in itself more profound than the Western-Slavophile dichotomy, and it should be based on the intertextual content of their works. In this sense a poet printing perfectly genuine verse about his native village and his peasant ancestors in the journal *Molodaia gvardiia* may be a considerably less Russian poet than an out-and-out town-dweller with 'alien' origins and subject-matter that is intellectual and cosmopolitan. Of course, quite the reverse could also be the case. Everything is determined by the discourse of the given poet, the *slovo* in Bakhtin's understanding: the deeper and broader the link between the poet's discourse and all the Russian poetry that has gone before, moreover, not only in the matter of quotation, but in all respects, including rhythm, intonation and sound-structure, then the more he is a Russian poet.

Thus Iosif Brodskii and a companion of his poetic youth like Nikolai Rubtsov are Russian poets to an identical degree, notwithstanding all the differences in their biographies and subject-matter. Differentiation takes place on other levels, specifically on two: on the level of self-definition of the poetic persona (the lyric hero) in relation to his motherland, and on the figurative-thematic level, that is, what system of word images the poet develops for the description of his native land.

It is instructive to compare Brodskii and Rubtsov because, while belonging to the same poetic generation (in terms of chronology and their circle of acquaintances), they are perceived, at least by admirers of the late Rubtsov, as antagonists. This is a superficial perception, a comparison not of their verse, but their lives: Brodskii was a town-dweller from a Jewish intellectual family, Rubtsov an orphan from the countryside who grew up in a children's home. But at the beginning of their careers, in the period of their poetic self-definition (the late 1950s and early 1960s), they had common friends, common readers and audiences. The style of each reflected certain common features characteristic of unofficial Leningrad poetry. It is as a result of this that there are textual echoes which from today's point of view are so unexpected. Rubtsov: '*Vse oblaka nad nei, vse oblaka . . ./ V pyli vekov mgnovenny i nezrimy/ Idut po nei, kak prezhde, piligrimy . . .*' ('Staraia doroga').[14] Brodskii: '. . . *idut po zemle/ piligrimy*' ('Piligrimy', *SIP*, 66); compare also '*Proplyvaiut oblaka*' (*OVP*, 70). Rubtsov: '*Ia budu skakat' po kholmam zadremavshei otchizny . . .*' (131). Brodskii: '*Ty poskachesh' vo mrake po besk-rainym kholodnym kholmam . . .*' (*OVP*, 43). Rubtsov: '*Gde-to poslyshitsia penie detskogo khora . . .*' (290) and '. . . *i pen'ia net, no iasno slyshu ia/ Nezrimykh pevchikh pen'e khorovoe . . .*' (17). Brodskii: '*Slyshis' li, slyshish' li ty v roshche detskoe penie . . .*' (*OVP*, 70). Incidentally, this motif of hidden music, the Muse, archaic when set against Leningrad avant-gardism of that time, is very characteristic of both poets. Also characteristic of both is the realisation of their natural exceptionality. In order to cite their most direct utterances on this subject, we have to compare quotations from works in dissimilar genres. 'Overflowing fullness of feeling is the most valuable quality of a verse . . .', wrote Rubtsov (7). Brodskii in one of the 'serious' passages of his wickedly funny poem 'Dva chasa v rezervuare' wrote: '*Odnako chelovek, main libe gerren,/ nastol'ko v sil'nykh chuvstvakh neuveren,/ chto pominutno lzhet . . .*'. And later on: '*Di Kunst gekhapt potrebnost' v pravde chuvstva*' (*OVP*, 163).

Rubtsov, who posthumously became a classic of Russian 'Neoslavo-philism', and Brodskii, who from the latter's point of view is not organic, is alien to Russian culture, belonged to a single poetic generation, a single poetic circle, wrote in the first period of their careers in a single poetic language, and much that was said by the 'Slavophile' Rubtsov could have been said by the 'Westerniser' Brodskii and *vice versa*.

But among Rubtsov's utterances there are those which could not be imagined coming from Brodskii's pen. This is from memoirs about Rubtsov: '. . . near the very end of his service (in the navy) the poet said with sadness: "For four years the petty-officer has racked his brains over how to keep me clothed and fed. Now I'll have to rack my own . . ."' (8). It would be possible not to ascribe great characterological significance to this light-hearted remark, if it did not have so much in common with the most personal, the most 'Rubtsovian' notes in Rubtsov's poetry. Rubtsov's most ardent apologist, V. Kozhinov, quite rightly distinguishes as the chief quality of his poetry 'its ability to elicit a sense of the verse having appeared spontaneously, unaided, from no origins' (Introduction, 16). Indeed, Rubtsov is distinguished even from his beloved Esenin by the complete absence of a self-portrait in his verse, the total merging of the authorial personality with the crowd and the landscape, so that it is unclear whether he endows them with his own wistful and emotional experiences, or whether they (birches, clouds, 'kind Filia') speak with his voice. Brodskii spells out as a matter of particular pride: '*Moia pesnia byla lishena motiva,/ no zato ee khorom ne spet*' (*KPE*, 106).

Quoted particularly often are Rubtsov's lines:

S kazhdoi izboiu i tucheiu,
S gromom, gotovym upast',
Chuvstvuiu samuiu zhguchuiu,
Samuiu smertnuiu sviaz'. (142)

This is the end of the poem 'Tikhaia moia rodina'. Rubtsov's meditation on the theme of his own poetic genesis takes the following shape in terms of subject: the poet returns to his native region after a long absence, recalls his childhood, notes the changes since then (many for the worse: '*Kupol tserkovnoi obiteli/ Iarkoi travoiu zaros*' and '*Tina teper' i bolotina/ Tam, gde kupat'sia liubil . . .*' [141]), and closes the poem with the vivid stanza cited above, which in turn has its culmination at the end, even in the very last word – *sviaz'* (union). Formally, this poem belongs to a legion of similar nostalgic, patriotic outpourings. Every detail of the landscape being described is drawn from those that are traditionally popular with the public: willows, nightingales, the mother's grave, the old schoolhouse, the expanse of green. Even the grass on the church dome is *bright*. In other words, in Lermontov's words, there is nothing *strange* in this love for the homeland, this is a *natural* love, or, as the young Brodskii would have expressed it, 'a hymn to the banal'. Rubtsov overcomes banality with his musicality: the sound-painting, the intonational structure of this poem are so unobtrusively perfect that the emotions presented therein seem to have been expressed for the first time.

In Brodskii's work the theme of the homeland and origins is presented differently, with the use of images of a diametrically opposed character:[15]

Ia rodilsia i vyros v baltiiskikh bolotakh, podle
serykh tsinkovykh voln, vsegda nabegavshikh po dve,
i otsiuda – vse rifmy, otsiuda tot bleklyi golos,
v'iushchiisia mezhdu nimi, kak mokryi volos,
esli v'etsia voobshche. (ChR, 83)

For Rubtsov the nostalgic landscape, the landscape of memory, is even more beautiful than the present one: '*Tina teper' i bolotina/ Tam, gde kupat'sia liubil . . .*'. For Brodskii his native region is unattractive to begin with – '*baltiiskie bolota*'. Rubtsov uses vivid colours – '*iarkaia trava*', '*novyi zabor*'. Brodskii has '*serye tsinkovye*'. The collection of traditional, attractive, song-like images of Rubtsov is contrasted with the markedly degrading 'unaesthetic' comparison of Brodskii's own voice (in both senses – the physical voice and the poetic voice, the style) with a wet hair (what is more, the rhyme '*golos-volos*' is familiar from extremely vulgar folklore). Rubtsov writes in a highly melodious, regular dactyl, with a single subtle omission of a syllable ('syncopation') in the first line; Brodskii in accented lines (*dol'nik*), approaching in their intonational structure the broken rhythm of the spoken language. The resolution of the theme 'the native land and I' is the same for both poets and consists in their acknowledgement of the complete determination of their own personality by their place of birth. Their attitude to their birthplace is also identical – they feel gratitude and love. There, in Brodskii's words, the heart is protected from insincerity. The difference, as we can see, lies in the system of describing the homeland, in their means of description. In contrast to Rubtsov, Brodskii does not decorate his poetic vision of his native region with a choice of predominantly positive epithets, he does not create a moving intonation, he does not give a pathos-laden declaration of love and, finally, does not select from the surroundings only attractive details pleasing to the eye, but rather seems to inform his poetic vision with the objectivity of a cine-camera, capturing everything in turn: a canvas of curtains, a shutter, the palm of a hand, 'a kettle boiling on an oil-stove', seagulls.

This sort of enumeration, nomination as a poetic device, is very characteristic of Brodskii's poetics. It is precisely thus that it blends the principles of Acmeism and Eliot's objective correlative. Brodskii speaks of art with assuredness: '*osnovnoi ego zakon,/ bessporno, nezavisimost' detalei*' (*OVP*, 118). Also 'independent' of the poet's feelings are the details which help him to recreate in his verse the object of his *strange* love, his motherland. But as just such an 'independent detail' in his work, there also appears man in the landscape, the author. For self-description Brodskii chooses emphatically objective word-images: '*chelovek*', '*telo*'. He uses them very consistently. Rubtsov's union, a metaphorical unbreakable umbilical cord, is absent in this world of independent objects and bodies. Rubtsov's basically collectivistic view of the world seeks to subjugate reality, to colour and harmonise it with uplifting emotion. Brodskii's individualistic view of the world cannot permit itself such weakness or, from his point of view, falsity. This human and artistic position can be expressed very simply: There is no reason to be proud of love for one's motherland – it is within you independent of yourself. It is not exactly irrational, but simply genetically implanted in your personality. Freedom is not an easy, but an unavoidable and conscious choice. When it has been made, it is not right to feel sorry for yourself.

III

At the heart of the way Brodskii describes the West lies a paradoxical, oxymoronic combination of concreteness and extreme – here one can use a Biblical definition – 'formlessness' ('*bezvidnost'*'). All that he sees around him he sees with his former, if not greater, keenness. In an anonymous small town in America is a '*kafe s opushchennoiu shtoroi,/ kirpichnyi bank s rasplastannym orlom*' (*ChR*, 29). In Venice there are '*gnilye svai*', '*shpili, kolonny, rez'ba, lepnina*' (*ChR*, 41, 42). In London there are '*bank[i] s sodoi v stekle apteki*', '*verenitsa barzh*', '*avtobus u galerei Teit*' (*ChR*, 46). In Florence there is the Old Bridge on which '*boiko torguiut vsiacheskoi branzuletkoi*', '*zolotye priadi skloniaiushcheisia za redkoi/ veshch'iu krasavitsy, roiushcheisia mezh korobok/ pod nesytymi vzgliadami molodykh torgovok*' (*ChR*, 111-12), dirty marble, a tub with a verbena. These are lines from the poems 'Osennii vecher v skromnom gorodke', 'Laguna', 'Temza v Chelsi' and 'Dekabr' vo Florentsii'. Considerably more could be quoted from each of them. At times, as in several sections of 'Meksikanskii divertisment', for example, the subject of the poem is confined to the enumeration of things seen.

On the other hand, the general tone of the foreign landscapes created by Brodskii is precisely one of formlessness, anonymity and colourlessness. Here, for instance, are the sort of epithets that mount up in the elegy 'Temza v Chelsi': *dingy, grey, endless, brown,* once more *grey, colourless,* once more *colourless.* Predominant in the landscape of Venice, naturally, is *dead* water on which *no traces are left.* But even on the dry land of Florence in the centre of the composition is the river, the embankment, a bridge, and the colouring is dampness, greyness: the doors of houses *'vydykhaiut par'*, *'syrye sumerki'*, the dank cavity of a gateway, a dusty coffee-house, dirty marble.[16]

What is also characteristic of these pieces is the rarity with which 'I' appears in them. In places where it could appear there predominate impersonal or indefinite personal constructions: *'Zdes' mozhno zhit', zabyv pro kalendar''*, *'i kogda v nem spish''*, *'nevozmozhno zhit', ne pokazyvaia kulaka'* and so on. Alternatively the form of expression in the first person is replaced by expression in the third person: moreover this third person is referred to with emphasised anonymity, like the most insignificant character listed in the *dramatis personae* of some play. *'Chelovek v plashche'* is found in 'Laguna' and again in 'Temza v Chelsi', but even this seems to the author too personal, and in 'Dekabr' vo Florentsii' there appears *'telo v plashche'*. One comes across simply *'telo'*, too: *'telo syplet shagi na zemliu . . .'* ('Temza v Chelsi'). The face of this 'third person' is *'kak skomkannaia bumaga'* ('Dekabr' vo Florentsii').

Another word which Brodskii substitutes for 'I' is 'Nobody'. In 'Laguna' it is put quite bluntly: *'sovershennyi nikto' (ChR,* 40). In 'Na smert' druga' is 'the anonymous author' (*'imia reku tebe . . . ot menia, anonima'* [*ChR,* 31]). The hero of Brodskii's lyric verse of wandering (specifically lyric verse, and not poetic novellas like '1867' in 'Meksikanskii divertisment') is a faceless personality, deprived of the capacity to identify with his surroundings and thus to be fulfilled. We are dealing with the existential tragedy not so much of freedom of choice as of the choice of freedom. Hence the dramatic tension of these poems, which the reader cannot possibly understand on a mundane level. Thus E. Limonov sees here just the journal, devoid of inspiration, of a traveller luckier (read: richer) than himself.[17]

In Brodskii's mythopoeia Nobody is undoubtedly not only a pro-noun, but also a name. Odysseus called himself Nobody to save himself from the vengeance of Polyphemus, whom he had blinded.[18] In the poem written on the threshold, and with the presentiment, of exile, 'Odissei Telemaku' (1972), the central motif is already dis-orientation in historical time (*'Troianskaia voina/ okonchena. Kto pobedil – ne pomniu'* [*ChR*, 23]) and space (*'Mne neizvestno, gde ia nakhozhus'* . . .' and later on *'vse ostrova pokhozhi drug na druga,/ kogda tak dolgo stranstvuesh'* [Ibid.]). Later in the same year Brod-skii finds himself in reality *'v neznakomoi mestnosti'* ('1972') and sends letters into the past (to a dead addressee!) he sends *'s beregov neizvestno kakikh'* (*ChR*, 31) or *'niotkuda s liubov'iu'* (*ChR*, 77).

Nobody lives in Nowhere, where the Gospel is replaced by a tautological absurd (*'pokuda est' pravyi bereg u Temzy, est'/ levyi bereg u Temzy. Eto – blagaia vest'* [*ChR* 48]), where it is possible to convince oneself of one's own existence or the cessation of the same only by fortuitous, unreliable, indirect evidence:

Potomu chto kabluk ostavliaet sledy – zima . . . (*ChR* 81)
Zdes' utrom, vidia skisshim moloko,
molochnik uznaet o vashei smerti. (*ChR*, 30)
. . . mozhno, gliadia v gazetu, stolknut'sia so
stat'ei o prokhozhem, popavshem pod koleso;
i tol'ko naidia abzats o tom, kak skorbit rodnia,
s oblegchen'em podumat': eto ne pro menia. (*ChR*, 47)

What a difference in the past. There the existence of the lyric hero was confirmed by love. He was the object of love and therefore existed.

(Ia znal, chto ia sushchestvuiu,
poka ty byla so mnoiu.) (*ChR*, 67)
Ia byl tol'ko tem, chego
ty kasalas' ladon'iu . . . (*NSKA*, 145)

At times the lyric hero feels himself in a state of at least secret war with the surrounding minus-territory. *'Ia . . . shpion, lazutchik, pia-taia kolonna/ gniloi tsivilizatsii* . . .' (*ChR*, 28). In 'Barbizon terras', the hotel in which *I*, in this instance *'chelovek v korichnevom'*, is staying is compared with the Trojan horse. 'The man in brown' finds that:

Krov' v viskakh
stuchit, kak ne priniatoe nikem
i vernuvsheesia vosvoiasi morze. (*U*, 38)

There is one exception in the deeply negative, chaotic, unsubstantiated geography of the West. That is Rome. The true site of that same 'rotten civilisation' of which Brodskii felt himself a spy amid the suburbia of the Middle West, Rome is the 'place of man in the universe' in Mandel'shtam's well-known expression. The entire cycle of 'Rimskie elegii' and the poem 'P'iatstsa Mattei' stand out among Brodskii's Western verse by virtue of their buoyancy of personal feeling: powerful here are the motifs of joyful flesh, sun, religious gratitude; that is, here is something diametrically opposed to the unpleasant incorporeality, the grey, misty colouring and the absurd 'symbol of faith' of the pieces discussed above.

The continuity with Mandel'shtam is emphasised by the closing lines of the 'Rimskie elegii'. Speaking quite plainly in the first person, the author says that he has been happy. Everything here is in contrast to his other pictures of the West. Even that rarest of punctuation marks in Brodskii's work, the exclamation mark, appears in these joyful lines. And they end with a direct paraphrase of Mandel'shtam:

Ia byl v Rime. Byl zalit svetom. Tak,
kak tol'ko mozhet mechtat' oblomok!
Na setchatke moei – zolotoi piatak.
Khvatit na vsiu dlinu potemok. (*U*, 116–17)

(Compare with Mandel'shtam's: '*I svoimi kosymi podoshvami/ Luch stoit na setchatke moei*': 'Stikhi o neizvestnom soldate').[19]

In Rome the Russian poet feels himself at home. This sensation stems from the cultural tradition of the nineteenth century, but above all from Mandel'shtam himself, who literally ended his poetic career with lines expressing his aspiration:

Ot molodykh eshche voronezhskikh kholmov
K vsechelovecheskim – iasneiushchim v Toskane.[20]

Mandel'shtam's last epithet, *universally human*, is taken, of course, from the poetic lexicon of Dostoevskii.[21] In these verses the Western-Slavophile dichotomy is removed. The Russian poet is universally human. Russian civilisation is inseparably linked with that of Europe. In his Roman poems Brodskii is a Russian poet who has successfully made his way to his spiritual ancestral homeland, Rome. He has completed a pilgrimage which those he chose as his poetic ancestors, Batiushkov, Pushkin, Baratynskii and Mandel'shtam, did not manage to complete, and he is happy.

Translated by Galya and Hugh Aplin

NOTES

1. Iu.M. Lotman, *Struktura khudozhestvennogo teksta* (Moscow, 1969), p. 282.
2. Quotations from Brodskii's verse are taken from the following editions: *Stikhotvoreniia i poemy* (New York, 1965) (*SIP*); *Ostanovka v pustyne* (New York, 1970) (*OVP*); *Konets prekrasnoi epokhi* (Ann Arbor, Michigan, 1977) (*KPE*); *Chast' rechi* (Ann Arbor, Michigan, 1977) (*ChR*); *Novye stansy k Avguste* (Ann Arbor, Michigan, 1983) (*NSKA*); *Uraniia* (Ann Arbor, Michigan, 1987) (*U*). References to these editions are given in the text by the abbreviated title followed by the page number.
3. A.S. Pushkin, *Sobranie sochinenii v desiati tomakh*, 3rd edition (Moscow, 1962–6), VI, p. 671.
4. Recently Soviet additions have been made to the numerous Western publications about the persecution suffered by Brodskii in his youth and about the 1964 trial. The most detailed and authentic account of these events is in Ia. Gordin's essay 'Delo Brodskogo', *Neva*, 2, 1989, pp. 134–66.
5. For a more detailed discussion see my article 'Poetics/Politics', in L. Loseff and V. Polukhina (eds), *The Poetics and Aesthetics of Joseph Brodsky* (London, 1990), pp. 34–55.
6. B. Paramonov, 'Sovetskoe evraziistvo', *Novoe russkoe slovo*, 22 August 1989, p. 5.
7. Ibid.
8. S.A. Esenin, *Sobranie sochinenii v piati tomakh* (Moscow, 1966–8), II, p. 119.
9. A.A. Blok, *Sobranie sochinenii v vos'mi tomakh* (Moscow-Leningrad, 1960–63), III, p. 306.
10. V.A. Sollogub, *Povesti i rasskazy* (Moscow-Leningrad, 1962), p. 164.
11. A.A. Fet, *Moi vospominaniia* (Moscow, 1890), p. 299.
12. *An Age Ago: A Selection of Nineteenth-Century Russian Poetry*, selected and translated by Alan Myers with a foreword and biographical notes by Joseph Brodsky (Harmondsworth, 1989), pp. xvi–xvii.
13. Fet, op. cit., p. 299.
14. N. Rubtsov, *Stikhi* (Moscow, 1986). Introduction by V. Kozhinov. Page references to this edition are given in the text.
15. A traditionally sentimental treatment of the motif of nostalgia is found in Brodskii's early poems, of which 'Stansy' is particularly popular ('*Ni strany, ni pogosta . . .*': *SIP*, 63).
16. It is interesting to compare Brodskii's Florence with that of Blok in the famous cycle 'Florentsiia' ('*Gniloi morshchinoi grobovoiu/ Iskazheny tvoi cherty!*' and so on): Blok, op. cit., III, pp. 106–9.

17. E. Limonov, 'Poet-bukhgalter. (Neskol'ko iadovitykh nabliudenii po povodu fenomena I.A. Brodskogo)' in the album *Muleta A* (Paris, 1984), pp. 133–5. Limonov writes:

> Brodskii's exile is an exile that is imposing, stylish, decadent, an exile for people of means. Geographically it is Venice, it is Rome, it is London, it is the museums, churches and streets of the capitals of Europe. It is good hotels, from the windows of which can be seen not a peeling wall in New Jersey, but the Venetian lagoon. Brodskii alone out of hundreds of Russian émigré poets is able to maintain a standard of living which allows him to think, travel and, if he really must get angry, then with the universe (etc.). (135)

In this extract the author himself is more interesting than what he writes about Brodskii. For Limonov, unfamiliar names like San Pietro or East Finchley sound, to use his language, 'imposing, stylish'. Also interesting is his conviction that only a certain 'standard of living' allows one to think and get angry with the universe alone.

18. 'Nobody' is also the pseudonym of Innokentii Annenskii, the forefather of the Petersburg school of poetry which Brodskii revived.
19. O. Mandel'shtam, *Voronezhskie tetradi* (Ann Arbor, Michigan, 1980), p. 93.
20. Ibid., p. 62.
21. See *Podrostok*, Part III, Chapter 7, and, of course, the Pushkin speech.

5 Residents and Refugees
Vasilii Aksenov

Mandel'shtam once said that Russian literature was born under the 'star of scandal'. Soviet literature has lived, from the 1920s onwards, under the sign of congestion. Ideological congestion was aggravated by the housing crisis. From the very start writers were drawn to one another, grouped together in various 'palaces of the arts' and literary settlements, naively supposing that intellectuals would not harm one another. It was in these very places that the fundamental betrayals were initiated. This tradition lives on in the Soviet Union to the present day; one only has to recall the accumulations of writers near the metro station Aeroport in Moscow, in Peredelkino and on the Pakhra.

The claustrophobia of a closed society and the life of the communal flats to which it gave rise were in many ways the inspiration of Bulgakov's satire as a genre. In an area covering eleven time-zones the regime contrived to create an unimaginable crush of people, a heap of pitiful belongings, a labyrinth of Kafkaesque corridors and dead-ends.

Suffocating from claustrophobia, Bulgakov threw open the walls of the communal flats into different dimensions, into the depths of the unknown. In practical life, after an unsuccessful attempt to emigrate, he none the less sought to find a place for himself – in the writers' restaurant, the billiards-room, the airless literary section of the Moscow Arts Theatre, he sought to mask his refugee essence.

Mandel'shtam did not so much as try to don a mask. Even on the Soviet railways, where it was not wanderings but the transportation of the masses that was taking place, he hung his bundle on an artificial palm-tree and said to Akhmatova: 'The wanderer is in the desert'. As long as he could, he fled to the south, to his ontological homeland. Escape to the expanse of the Mediterranean is his favourite theme. He never really settled down in Russia – he was either accompanying his swallows in their flight across the sea to Egypt, or wandering across Rovenna with his sheep in the dusk, or else slipping among the Achaean ships in their crane-like wedge formation . . . All this movement towards the Mediterranean, the joy of migration, the scents of ancient hearths, the wars of the Bronze

Age – all are symbols of escape from Soviet Russian claustrophobia, attempts to avoid being crammed into terminal overcrowding, into the sleeve of a stifling, and evidently stinking, 'fur-coat of the Siberian steppes'.

And only when surrounded, as in Vysotskii's wolf-hunt, did the poet seem prepared to lay down the laurels of his constant flight, give up the title of wolf and pretend to be a hat – 'shove me in properly, like a hat into a sleeve'. But even here, even here he still looks to climb out through some tear into the starry night, to the flow of the Enisei; that is, once more, none the less, to make a dash for it. And that was how he died, in the wide expanses, without ever learning about agoraphobia.

In the literature of the post-Stalin period there was a struggle between two principles – claustrophobia and agoraphobia. Despite ever more frequent attempts to push the walls aside and burst out into the open, the latter principle was to a huge degree still predominant.

It is above all the sense of belonging that makes conformism cosy. When you reach a certain level of recognition and are considered to have become part of the 'national heritage' – Lenin's definition of your personal talent – there appears within you a really quite nice state of balance: conformism is comfort. On the one hand you are gratified by the illusion of freedom from surveillance; the KGB strolls by, albeit within view, but at a respectful distance. On the other hand you are protected from excessively open expanses, where agoraphobia can turn you into a worthless reed and no intoxicating ecstasy in freedom will provide recompense for what you have lost.

However, it was precisely for this intoxicating ecstasy, for the conquest of fear and for the boundless expanse of flight that Russian romanticism has longed from Kheraskov onwards, although the box-rooms of belonging have constantly whispered to it – 'don't be stupid'.

You could not find a better battlefield for these two principles than Nikolai Vasil'evich Gogol'. He was always seeking to escape and at the same time was always seeking to hide. These motivations are represented most clearly in his two masterpieces that are such poles apart, *Nos* and *Shinel'*. In the one we see the olfactory organ in free flight, in predatory search, escaping; while in the other we are all but lulled to sleep by the scratching of pens in office corners, all but burst into sobbing over the saving of coppers towards that eternally warm refuge, the greatcoat, the symbol of belonging.

The romanticism which the Bolsheviks could not entirely quash, and which was reborn in the 1960s, immediately began to show signs of agitation and to fidget in the kangaroo pouch of the CPSU. The theme of life abroad, the dream of crossing the frontier began to flicker across our pages, at times, it should be added, besmirching them by our age-old Russian habit of sentimentalising. Yet leaving aside sentimentality of any sort, it can be asserted that life abroad became the great dream of a generation, a generation that had been processed from childhood with a view to making it the first generation of ideal Socialist citizens, grateful even for being allowed to live.

Berdiaev wrote somewhere that any journey abroad is a breakthrough from so-called reality into the unknown. But having lived the greater part of his life in the open society of old Russia and democratic Europe, he probably could not fully imagine how right he would be in respect of succeeding generations of Soviets.

Every Soviet traveller has experienced that strange feeling of approaching the frontier as though it were the border not of a country, but of life, or even existence in general.

It is hard to believe fully – will it really happen, will I really find myself outside the USSR? Everything *beyond* is filled with particular meaning, everything seen and heard makes an impression, the senses become more acute, as if after smoking marijuana, time, each moment of which is imbued with special significance, expands, yet is at the same time condensed, reality is experienced with exceptional keenness and none the less seems to be make-believe.

In August 1976 my mother, Evgeniia Ginzburg, and I were travelling by rail from Moscow to Paris. How we managed to extract our visas from Auntie Stepanida is another story, but, one way or another, my mother, an old inmate of the camps, whose best years were spent in the extreme claustrophobia of the Gulag, was for the first time approaching the state frontier without believing in the miracle for one single moment. 'You can tell me whatever you like', she kept repeating, 'but this is not possible. I – abroad? Rubbish!'

After we had crossed the Soviet-Polish frontier we began our approach towards a still more important border, the frontier of the Socialist bloc. The train dragged slowly through East Berlin, stopping frequently; the Prussian guards appeared with their leaden eyes, demanded: '*Ihre Papiere*'. Then we began to pass by totally empty platforms. Prussian guards with automatics still loomed in places, but they soon disappeared as well.

Mama, pale and almost triumphant, stood at the window and kept on glancing at me, as if to ask: 'Now? Now?'. Even I, who had crossed this sacred zone many times before, was excited.

For a time it was difficult to decide whether it was already the West or still the East, until there appeared on one of the platforms the figure of a tall, thin old man in a long tweed coat with two dachshunds on leads. I told Mama that this at last was a resident of the West with two Western dogs just waiting for their train. She kept her eyes fixed on this melancholy trio for a long time. It never occurred to the old man, of course, what a subtext he was endowed with by passengers in the passing Moscow-Paris train.

Becoming permanent residents in the West, we have lost these subtexts and also the magic of crossing the frontier.

There was a period when I was given no peace by an absurd marshbird, a heron. I was living at the time on the shores of the Baltic in a restricted area and could see this bird flying nightly into Poland. The notion of the free passage of a bird across the frontier aroused in me such an intense metaphysic that it engendered a certain long-legged symbol of the young girl Europa, which roamed from one book of mine to the next until it ended up in a dramaturgical paraphrase of Chekhov's *Chaika*.

The romanticism of the first rebellious Soviet generation in the 1970s finally settled in the West. Belgium seemed a country of greater exoticism and space than Mongolia. Of America nothing needs to be said: the address 'Peoria, Illinois' rang out like a silver trumpet. One Moscow prose-writer enjoyed repeating, always inappositely, the word 'Minnesota'. Once I asked what it signified for him. Nothing, he confessed, just some hopeful whistling, the last chance, as it were.

Having settled in the West, we have evidently ceased to experience the metaphysic of this 'minnesota'. A quite natural demythologisation has taken place of many formerly cherished symbols. One would have thought that the bastard offspring of Socialism would have been dizzy from the space, and the opposite feeling to claustrophobia might have developed: for there is too much of the *agora* around, the intoxicating expanse of world literature, the singing of sirens beneath the waves and beneath the heavens – block up my ears with wax, or else I shall lose my head in rapture.

However, this feeling quickly evaporated along with the initial euphoria of being like a tourist. At a certain moment the refugee suddenly notices that here too, surprise, surprise, it is just a little crowded.

I have already written of how the image of Western literature is deromanticised in the eyes of an émigré from Russia or Eastern Europe. At first, of course, he is delighted when the stereotypes of which he has dreamed are confirmed: the government here does not set up any obstacles for literature and, what is more, has not the slightest influence upon it! After a short while, however, he notices that literature is entirely divided up between literary agencies, and realises that he too needs to find himself a kind Dutch uncle as quickly as possible.

Yet there would appear to be no gain from these uncles, on the contrary, only losses; but without them nothing can be achieved. Ideologically free literature is commercially well-organised. The names of authors and the titles of books roll silently through the world literary computer like wheat, beef and other commodities through the Chicago stock exchange. It all vibrates in synchronised harmony: if less copies of your last novel were sold, you will receive a smaller advance on your next book. Cover the advance and earn a little more – what do you know, your value is increased. All is fair, all is natural; the market, ladies and gentlemen. The market knows exactly what size of advertisement should be allotted to your book and where it should be placed – in the middle of a weekly or nearer the periphery; whether to display your book in the shop-window; whether to turn the front cover to face shoppers or to slip it in sideways among countless other spines.

A friend of mine, a publisher, telephoned me one day. 'Listen', he said excitedly, '*Publishers' Weekly* has given you an amazing review. I'm sending it to you by express post.' The next morning I received the review and found nothing special in it. I told my friend about this. 'But don't you understand', he replied in vexation, 'it was printed in the top left-hand corner of the page, and besides, you are compared in it to Tom Wolfe.'

'So is there really any similarity with Tom Wolfe?' I asked.

'Well, I don't know', sighed my friend, 'but if you were ever to sell even one quarter of what Tom Wolfe sells . . .'

Not only on the approaches to the Olympus of the best-seller list can it be quite crowded. A refugee or exile from Russia or Eastern Europe begins to notice that in the West, too, writers show a liking for grouping together and seek the comfort of belonging, if only to that inevitable Left-Liberal tendency. The refugee himself soon begins to look around in search of a shoulder to lean on.

But this is not so simple. The refugee did not expect rapturous noises in connection with his arrival, yet nor did he expect utter indifference. He in turn, at first in anger, deliberately, then more and more naturally, becomes indifferent to his Western colleagues.

Initially he continues to tell himself: okay, their experience is familiar to me, if not through their writing, then through what is written about them; while my experience is unknown to them; but because they are not aware of it, or do not want to learn of it, it does not become any less significant for me.

That grandiose event in the life of a refugee, his escape, remains his alone, but is none the less a tremendously serious possession, his orgy of freedom, after which everything seems to him rather insipid.

Then, becoming increasingly alienated and indifferent, the refugee begins to understand the laws of 'understatement', the wisdom of university seminars and workshops, and does not notice himself as he ceases to be a refugee and willy-nilly himself becomes a resident, a Western writer.

Does this mean he is permanently cured of his liking for flight? By no means. He escaped to the West not because he was from the East, but because he was an escaper. From time to time he sees a kindred light shining in someone's eyes on the periphery of the much-loved ego, and then he realises that there are no 'Easterners' and 'Westerners', but only 'the settled' and 'the wandering'. Groups and loners.

The group lives according to the laws of the myth it has itself created; the loner roams about on his own, more often than not without formulating anything and with only a vague appreciation of the parameters of his code of morals or, more often still, of his feeling of style. One way or another, there develops within him a sort of ethic of not belonging.

The concept of Western literary success is also subject to deromanticisation in the eyes of the émigré. The myth of the untold intellectuality and sophistication of Western society is eroded even more quickly than the language barrier. The straightforward system of 'supply and demand', like the vicious circle of the mass literature market it spawns, becomes all too evident.

With despondency he notes the almost complete absence of experimentation, the fear of the avant-garde tradition, explained away more often than not with the pitiful excuse that 'it's all been done before'. He sees the strange absence of literary life: that is, even if there is no battle, at least there should be some scandal. The last slap in the face in American literature, he recalls, was delivered a good ten years ago.

The reason for all this caution, when it finally comes home to him, is astounding in its scantiness: the main thing is not to upset 'marketing', not to weaken one's chances of becoming a 'best-seller'.

Who needs our experiments and other literary tricks? We are not writing for connoisseurs, ladies and gentlemen; but for the broad popular masses, comrades, art, and all the more so because literature belongs to the people, who carry to the tills their hard-earned dollars, pounds, francs, marks and lira.

It is not only 'vulgar' commercial success that is subject to deromanticisation, but also so-called elitist, Olympic, Nobel success, that is, in terms of prizes. It demands no great effort to decode the systems by which the mediocre constantly come through to the highest awards.

The refugee who has broken through the walls of claustrophobia sees that it is perhaps even more crowded here than anywhere else, in the midst of the interaction between groups of belonging, skilfully suspended webs, Potemkin villages and tarted-up myths.

At a certain point the refugee starts to feel uncomfortable in front of the mirror. 'Oho', he says to himself, 'it looks as if I am already beginning to slip down into the warm folds here as well, "like a bug in a rug"; we seem to have fixed ourselves up here quite comfortably in all these living-rooms of ours, we already seem to be quite nervous about going out into too open a space, we already seem to prefer not to listen to the metaphors whistling out there. Do we have enough fuel left now even to write something other than what is expected of us by the publisher or literary agent?'

The time approaches for a new escape into the expanse of the novel. A seditious idea visits the refugee author: let success chase me, rather than me chasing success.

One day in the street a little beagle with a smart collar but without 'ID' latched onto us. We took him along with us and he lived with us for four days, sleeping on the ottoman and clearly enjoying himself, until he suddenly began to prepare once more for another escape. We named him Hobo and did not let him run away. But suddenly at this point he was identified by his owner. 'We called the dog Pastrami', he told us sadly, 'but your name is clearly more appropriate. He has already run away three times and is always looking to make a bolt for it. We don't know what he's looking for at all.'

To this parable should be added the fact that in Petersburg in 1913 the poets' cafes were called 'The Stray Dog' and 'The Comedians' Rest'. The notion of flight and a wandering life has always been inseparable from the avant-garde. The avant-garde has always sought – often not without a degree of hypocrisy – a certain allegorical refuge, while knowing perfectly well that its true element is allegorical flight. It is still the same now.

Translated by Galya and Hugh Aplin

6 Western Life as Reflected in Aksenov's Work before and after Exile
Arnold McMillin

Vasilii Aksenov appears to have settled in the West far more successfully than many of his Third-Wave contemporaries, somehow avoid-
ing the stockade mentality (or, indeed, reality) that has beset many,
and continuing to write productively and with undiminished creativity in the new environment of what he calls, parodying a Soviet cliché
familiar to all travellers, 'the capital of our non-fatherland, Hero-city
Washington D.C.'.[1] His positive attitude is summed up in a characteristically provocative article of 1984 suggesting that emigration is
the best condition for [Russian] literature,[2] or, rather more prosai-
cally, that one can 'get used' to the West (the title of his 1983
interview for the journal *Novyi amerikanets*[3]), although it may be
noted that he has also said that for a contemporary writer emigration
is a 'dizzying adventure'[4] and on one occasion compared the experience to 'attending one's own funeral'.[5]

This paper offers brief consideration of Aksenov's pre-exile writing
and experience before turning to his later, post-exile, novels,
Bumazhnyi peizazh (1983) and *Skazhi izium* (1985) and, in particular, his book of memoirs and reflections on America *V poiskakh
grustnogo bebi* (1987): these last three throw considerable light on
Aksenov's perceptions of the West both before and after exile. From
his earliest prose at the end of the 1950s and beginning of the 1960s
Aksenov, like several other representatives of *molodaia proza*,
seems to have been inspired by the West, no doubt as a contrast to,
and imaginary escape from, the prevailing ethos of Stepanida
Vlas'evna (aka *Sovetskaia vlast'*) or, indeed – in a classic example of
synecdoche – the 'huge pimply arse of socialist realism' that he refers
to in his article 'V avangarde - bez tylov'.[6] Even in his first novella
Kollegi (1961), the work least remote from socialist realism, the
heroes make extensive use of anglicisms as fashionable youth slang,

50

with expressions such as *'gud bai'*, *'Khello komrids'*, and *'veri vell'*. This tendency towards Westernism was to continue increasingly throughout his work of the 1960s and 1970s, the West figuring as an image of positive exoticism, be it a sophisticated Italian method of sharing cigarettes with a loved one or even the visit of a British aircraft carrier to Leningrad.[7]

On a less superficial level there is reverence for the ideal of American personal freedom which in one of the Magadan episodes of *Ozhog* (1969–75, published 1980) is identified by the semi-autobiographical Tolia von Steinbok with the John Wayne character of the Ringo Kid from the Hollywood classic *Stagecoach*:[8] in his youth Aksenov saw this film at least ten times (under the title *Puteshestvie budet opasnym*) and another American classic, *The Roaring Twenties*, at least fifteen times (this one under the title *Sud'ba soldata v Amerike*) (*Vpgb*, 19–20); in an interview Aksenov has also recalled queuing for a week to attend an American performance of *Porgy and Bess* (Możejko, 17). Jazz – hated by Fascists and Communists alike – was associated, particularly for young Soviet people of Aksenov's generation, with a potent image of the West as a place of unfettered freedom (in *Skazhi izium* the hero Ogorodnikov refers unequivocally to 'the trumpets of freedom',[9] having become, in Aksenov's own words, 'something more than music, it acquired an ideology or, rather, an anti-ideology' [*Vpgb*, 306]). The figure of a jazz musician appears in many, probably most, of Aksenov's works, and jazz figures throughout his writing both as a dominant thematic leitmotiv and as a stimulus to stylistic experiment from the mid-1960s onwards, most notably in *Stal'naia ptitsa* (1965, published 1977) and *Zolotaia nasha zhelezka* (1972, published in Russian 1980), two stories combining fantastic absurdist writing with realism which seem to imitate American jazz in their form and rhythm.[10]

Already far more sophisticated than most of his literary contemporaries, Aksenov was in 1975 invited to spend a year as a visiting professor in the University of Southern California at Los Angeles, an experience which, at the most obvious level, ensured that in 1980 he was far better prepared than most Third-Wave exiles for life abroad. In literary terms it produced *Kruglye sutki non-stop* (1976), not the first of his travel memoirs but easily the liveliest, combining – characteristically – realism and fantasy, the latter in the form of a so-called Typical American Adventure taking in a quest for a Californian *prekrasnaia dama*,[11] the Mafia, Las Vegas, a ghost town, the Wild West and the Carmel Jazz Festival. Elements of the life-style and,

particularly, psychology of Southern California would also seem to
have influenced the depiction of the streets of Rome as a place of
'permanent half-crazy carnival' in *Ozhog*,[12] or, indeed, the picture of
life on the imaginary Island of Crimea in the novel of that title which
he wrote between 1977 and 1979, and which appeared after the
Metròpol' scandal of 1979 and Aksenov's subsequent expatriation.
Here Crimea, though a surviving democracy, is also a 'symbol of
Western decadence'[13] inhabited by carefree lotus-eaters who do not
even recognise the significance of a massive bombardment by a
Soviet aircraft carrier, taking it to be just another TV spectacular.
Interestingly, the central character, millionaire playboy Andrei
Luchnikov, hankers after the shabby but intimate intellectual and
spiritual mateyness to be found in Soviet kitchens and beer halls,
Aksenov thus accurately anticipating the aspect of life for which
many of his Third-Wave compatriots would be most homesick in
exile.[14]

As with many of his generation, Aksenov's first impressions of
America were derived from films, scraps of music and information
over the Western radio, and not least, indeed, perhaps more than
anything else, the idealisation which is typically, albeit paradoxically,
produced by Soviet anti-American propaganda. In his case, however,
knowledge based on first-hand experience (which, he drily recalls
['Oz', 10], proved not entirely welcome to some of his new compatriots), renders the question of his change of perceptions on
settling in the West quite different from that of most other Third-
Wave writers.

Since 1980 Aksenov's impressions of America have been reflected
in a multiplicity of newspaper articles and interviews as well as in the
three post-exile books which have already been mentioned. In
Bumazhnyi peizazh the rather ineffectual hero Igor' Velosipedov
writes to Brezhnev to complain about the immense quantity of bumf
that floods his flat, and to make three small requests: for a small plot
of land, a motorcar, and a trip to Bulgaria; this letter has far-reaching
consequences, and in the last chapter of the novel Velosipedov
arrives in New York, expatriated after a spell in the camps as a
presumed dissident, where he is surprised to find '*vsiu nashu shoblu*'
already installed.[15] The more dynamic hero of *Skazhi izium*, Maks
Ogorodnikov, is the leader of a group of photographers who are
planning to publish illegally a collection of uncensored photographs,
a project which bears an unmistakable resemblance to Aksenov's
Metròpol' volume and the intrigues and débâcle associated with it.

Although the action of the novel mainly takes place in the Soviet Union, there are also chapters set in Berlin, Paris and New York, each of which adds something to our understanding of the way Aksenov views the West. *V poiskakh grustnogo bebi*, written to some extent as a prelude to Aksenov's first fully American novel,[16] is an unusual quasi-memoir which gives an entertaining and very full picture of the writer's life in America.

Aksenov's life as an exile in America began in California where the difference between a year's visit and permanent residence proved great; if the impressions of Aksenov's first (1975) visit to Los Angeles are colourfully reflected in his works of the late 1970s (nearly all of which had to await his exile before being published in America), as a resident he soon felt himself cut off from culture and, indeed, contemporary life:

> In 1975 when I landed here for my first, short, visit, I was carried away by the mythology of Southern California, and did not notice its reality. After several months of everyday life [however], I began to notice myself doing everything possible to avoid the gloomy thought that 'we were living in a backwater' (*Vpgb*, 75–6).

These reflections would seem to be related to the broader problem of America's isolationism and, indeed, provincialism, in matters ranging from sport to literature, to which Aksenov has often referred in his post-exile writing. For the simple Ivan Velosipedov in *Bumazhnyi peizazh* one of the first impressions of America was the pleasing revelation (via a TV advertisement) of the secret of beauty, namely the Oil of Olé, but he was soon to be beset by elaborately gloomy thoughts as his ideals evaporated:

> The object of my dreams had now entirely evaporated. Bikoz, friends, Bulgaria in my imagination was all the same a part of America, albeit an intellectually accessible part of totally inaccessible America, while now I simply live in this immense Bulgaria, that is, simply in America. So where is my longed-for BNR now? Perhaps it has now become for me the only, albeit intellectually, accessible part of Russia? (Bp, 171)

Most of Velosipedov's problems are less abstract than this obsession with Bulgaria. America, for example, turns out to have an even richer paperscape than Russia, producing as much junk mail and official documents in a week as the Soviet Union had done in a month, including registration for social security, the AAA club, Blue Cross and Blue Shield, the Book of the Month Club, an account with the Chemical Bank and (at the same bank) an Individual Retirement account and much else.

Unlike his hero, Aksenov could not say that he had not been warned. One of *his* first experiences in the West, recounted in the first pages of *V poiskakh grustnogo bebi*, was an unpleasant meeting in Italy with two very self-satisfied writers, one Italian, the other German; Aksenov seems to have been unlucky with the Germans he has met, and the writer here, Klaus Gabriel von Liederhofen, complete with proletarian spectacles in metal frames, makes no bones of his supercilious surprise that, having left the Soviet Union, Aksenov should plan to live in America, exchanging, in his words, 'one hell for another' (*Vpgb*, 6). He would seem to have much in common with the affluent Communist photographer, Joachim von Deretzki, with whom Ogorodnikov clashes memorably in one of the Berlin chapters of *Skazhi izium*, causing the German to brand his Soviet colleague with the unintended compliment of 'dissident' before flouncing out to his red Ferrari sports car (*Si*, 121–2). It is, however, another German in this novel, the East German Wolf Schlippenbach who pinpoints one of the most striking features of the West from an East European point of view. Asked by Ogorodnikov whether he plans to defect, he replies: 'I shall never clear off to the West. There are too many Communists there, Max' (*Si*, 73). Aksenov finds some support for this view at a PEN-Club meeting in New York where it is again two Germans, the well-known writers Hans Enzensberger and Günter Grass, who show the greatest degree of aggressive political naivety, the latter declaring that 'capitalism is no better than the GULAG system'.[17] What Ogorodnikov refers to as the 'left-wing totalitarian scum' (*Si*, 137) seems less extreme in America, but Aksenov has described mixed feelings after a naively enthusiastic peace picnic in Vermont where it proves difficult to find an audience for his real experience in a supposedly anti-militaristic society. As always, however, the view he takes is a moderate one. After meeting the peaceniks, for instance, he reflects: 'What can I prove to these people?', but goes on immediately: 'The paradox is that without their presence in America there would be no America' (*Vpgb*, 71).

More ironic is Aksenov's observation that 'Soviets and Americans alike are quite ignorant about each other, but American ignorance seems more active than Soviet ignorance' (*Vpgb*, 89). Unlike many

Third-Wave writers and other émigrés, however, Aksenov is far from condemning the West for not paying more attention to his wise words; whilst not underestimating the positive catalytic role of the new immigrants (particularly exiled writers) in breaking down America's endemic but diminishing provincialism, he has often expressed gratitude to the West for its hospitality and for teaching people who were certainly not slaves in their own country a new kind of freedom.

Before turning to the specifics of Aksenov's portrayal of the United States, one or two words about his expressed view of other countries. If the Third World is seen mainly from the point of view of how its erstwhile citizens negatively influence the quality of life in America (I deliberately ignore the colourful Katangan scenes in *Ozhog*), England is treated very mildly as a country with a rich history, as the centre of a possibly renascent empire, and as the repository of America's past.[18] Perhaps enough has been said about Germans, easily the worst of Aksenov's anti-Americans. In *Skazhi izium* Ogorodnikov's main physical reaction to Berlin is an elephantine urination in the street, comparable perhaps to the prolonged vomiting which overtakes him in Paris. The latter city does, however, also provoke from Ogorodnikov a sadly nostalgic reflection on the emigrant's lot:

> The strange languor of emigration: in Moscow you feel stifled, and it seems as if real life is passing you by; you break free, and again you are surrounded by the backwoods, because you have lost Moscow . . . (*Si*, 145)

Somewhat similarly, as Aksenov reflects in *V poiskakh grustnogo bebi*, just as a Jew had to leave Russia to become Russian, a Russian had to go to America to feel himself European (p. 31).

Aksenov's reaction to the physical aspects of America need not detain us long, though it is expressed in some memorable images. The chapter of *Skazhi izium* in which Ogorodnikov visits New York is entitled 'Mokhnatyi' (a local Russian version of Manhattan).[19] At the start of this chapter Ogorodnikov's host Efim Chetverkind characterises the Big Apple as follows: 'New York is like a man who get himself an elegant kheardu . . . sorry, what? well, a hairdo, but never wipes his bum, a dirty arse, get it? The city is being ruined by scum from the third world' (*Si*, 187). One small New York event that seems to have made a lasting impression, being described in three of

Aksenov's books (I quote it from the *Bumazhnyi peizazh* version) takes place near the Sheraton Hotel: 'A tall, dark-skinned beggar roller-skated up to an urn with a timid plant, pulled out his equipment and urinated – long live freedom!' (p. 176).

In Washington, where Aksenov now lives, the architecture is better and the filth less extreme, though he still finds a great contrast between the squalor of broken glass and rotting garbage on the one hand and the high living standards that Americans take for granted on the other, between the dismal goods delivery service and the sophisticated technology, between the appalling bureaucracy and rudeness of the immigration department and the friendliness and hospitality of neighbours and, indeed, of the great majority of people he meets in the universities and Kennan Center. Though no racist, Aksenov seems to share the not uncommon émigré view that the most degenerate elements of Western society derive from the least developed groups ('the lower the level of development, the higher the level of debauchery' – *Vpgb*, 113). To the Anglo-Saxons, on the other hand, he gives much more credit than do many expatriate Russians:

> Human groups who are not concerned with the problems of civilisation . . . are mainly concerned with their desire for the good life. The most refined forms of sexual perversion were born not in civilised society, but in groups of savages. Western civilisation, especially in its Anglo-Saxon form, is in reality the last bastion of common sense. (*Vpgb*, 113)[20]

What is the lot of an expatriate Russian artist or writer in the United States? The experiences of the photographer Chetverkind as related to Ogorodnikov might seem typical for many, *mutatis mutandis*, though certainly not for Aksenov himself, who is in constant demand: 'And lo, I appeared in the "union" with my works of genius, bravo, they say, genius, that's it – Mazer-Rassia! Three exhibitions on the trot, reviews in the large journals and – enough, no money, no orders' (*Si*, 188). Even for Aksenov, however, there is little local resonance (Washington is not, after all, New York) and the remote Soviet audience (which, unlike Zinov'ev, for instance,[21] he is far from idealising)[22] remains the main one, although it is not considered important if some elements of his recent works are not fully understood there.[23] Extrapolating further from *Skazhi izium*, we learn of the exaggerated authority of exalted individuals such as the idolised and arrogant émigré photographer Alik Konskii, whose imprimatur is deemed essential by the New York art world and, most importantly, by publishers. As his friend Doug Semigorski explains to Ogorodnikov: 'There are so many good photographs nowadays, Max, that society is obliged to develop for itself authorities so that they can develop opinion. Caman, friend, now you yourself have a chance to become an authority in this city' (*Si*, 197). Less restricting than this artificial domination of taste, but none the less rather sad, is the loss of excitement in publishing. Viktor Nekrasov put it well in 1984 when he said, 'The real problem is that now I write and I don't risk anything. So what I'm missing in the West is knowing that I'm courageous'.[24] After experiencing persecution and danger in his attempts to get his book (also called *Skazhi izium*) published, Ogorodnikov feels no excitement in safer circumstances: '"Cheese" in New York, in safety, in an extremely luxurious building – you'd think one would jump for joy, but somehow this does not "move" me, as if it was all in the order of things' (*Si*, 200). Even Velosipedov has a comparable problem, expressed in somewhat Kharmsian terms:

Alas, here for a Muscovite man there is present the lack of something important. Take beer for instance. It is present and even, one could say, in an unlimited variety of packaging, but, alas, there is absent the joy of getting it and the triumph of a successful hunt, when even sourish Zhiguli beer diluted by Sofa [Soviet power – ABMcM] seems to everyone a heavenly delight. (*Bp*, 171)[25]

The Russian emigration in America appears to be in a weak and scattered condition, which is symbolised for Aksenov by the somewhat pitiful monument to Peter Dement'ev in St Petersburg, Florida (*Vpgb*, 248). He has also found elements of *nevezhestvo* and *khanzhestvo* amongst his fellow countrymen abroad.[26] However, more of a shock than any of these phenomena has been American literary provincialism, manifested in, amongst other things, great conservatism of taste and concomitant hostility, or at any rate indifference, to the *avant-garde*. From the hidebound Russia of Khrushchev and Brezhnev the American literary scene had appeared to be one huge cosmopolitan playground, but from closer to it seems, on the contrary, to be imbued with 'features of a village shop – the search for a "cert", fear of risk, and panic at the word "experiment"' (*Vpgb*, 186). Another side of this provincialism has turned out to be a

snobbish indifference and (at least, initial) lack of interest: if something does not happen to be known (in this case modern Russian
literature) it tends to be deemed not worth knowing. However,
Aksenov finds far more to praise than to mock in the American
universities, and he credits them with an important role in social
progress, believing that in the sixties they played a valuable part in
what was a time of transformation for Russia and America alike, a
time when both countries began to emerge from different forms of
isolationism.

Despite the latter tendency, provincialism in many spheres of life
provided an initial shock and is still a recurrent theme in Aksenov's
writing about America:

From the Soviet Union Americans appeared to us as 'citizens of
the world', polyglots, cosmopolitans. In real life they turned out to
be for the most part locked up in their own country, on the
American planet. (*Vpgb*, 145)

A lack of interest in the outside world can, of course, take many
forms: sport, in particular the ignorance of world ice hockey and the
obsession with incomprehensible American football, produced a very
negative early impression on Aksenov, as did the almost ubiquitous
smell of peanut butter, popcorn and ketchup. Provincialism, moreover, seems infectious: for example, émigrés like Alik Konskii in
Skazhi izium close their eyes to what is going on in the Soviet Union.
As Ogorodnikov reflects bitterly, 'We talked about nothing but those
who had "gone away", but for them, it turns out, their Muscovite
friends were something like country cousins' (*Si*, 191). It should be
said, however, that – despite his initial scorn – Aksenov is aware of
being drawn into this provincialism, which turns out to be a not
wholly negative phenomenon (*Vpgb*, 186–7): 'Cosmopolitan pathos
evaporates, and not only in sport. Willy-nilly I am being drawn into
the immense (and the point is that it is immeasurably large) and
colourful world of American provincialism' (*Vpgb*, 152).

Aksenov's view of America as reflected in his writing is on the
whole one of faith and optimism. America is perceived as being not
only rich and powerful, but also generous, tolerant and humane, free
of xenophobia, and ready to lead the world – if not already doing so –
to a new age of liberalism built on what Aksenov has termed beneficial or even noble inequality. Faced with such conditions, however, Soviet man in American society is ill-prepared: 'In his

consciousness he holds onto for a long time dogmas which are rather stronger than the views of the pagans of New Guinea' (*Vpgb*, 111). Indeed, Aksenov himself wonders how America supports such a variety of opinions and passions:

> American society is unique. Every now and then you are shocked by the thought of what supports this huge conglomerate with such a small degree of limitations, with such tolerance of natural human passions, lofty and low alike. (*Vpgb*, 178–9)

But if at first Russian immigrants often find the radical differences of opinion in American society catastrophic, they usually come round to acceptance that: 'it is precisely on this variety of opinion that American power is founded, with its flexibility and interchangeability of parts' (*Vpgb*, 135).

What of the celebrated rottenness that plays such a large part in the Soviet image of the West? To say nothing of its 'mistiness, falseness and lies' in the charming words of Alik Gorodnitskii's notorious song? For all the rotting vegetables and urban decay, Aksenov provides a robust and largely plausible answer to the clichéd charge: there is no time for Western society to rot, as the population is too busy in the 'useful, respectable and socially beneficial business' of making money (Możejko, 25):

> It [i.e. American society] has no intention of declining, decaying or falling into decadence. It simply has not the time for it. With frantic energy it is making money, money, money, and as a result of this unworthy, disgraceful business there grow up skyscrapers such as are not to be seen in the old world, the country is girded with an unbelievable network of freeways, and the workers, instead of making revolution, buy motor cars. (*Vpgb*, 13)

Although neither *Bumazhnyi peizazh* nor *Skazhi izium* have the exotic colouration of, for example, *Kruglye sutki non-stop*, *Ozhog* or *Ostrov Krym*, they none the less differ from Aksenov's non-fiction by the extremities of situation into which Velosipedov and Ogorodnikov get themselves, the latter seeking cover from the KGB in West Berlin from an unwitting American patrol jeep, Velosipedov – to give a second example – joining an American country hick who is being chased through the streets of New York by an unsavoury mob who, having already debagged him, are thirsting for still more excitement.

Aksenov's fiction and his non-fiction, which, indeed, often over-
lap, offer a lively, revealing and, above all, balanced picture of his
new homeland. As he himself realises, it is precisely from such
unhysterical emigrants that the West can learn how to deal with
Russia in the future.[27] Life in America has provided no more 'typically American adventures', but, taken as a whole, his recent consistently entertaining writing provides an ironic and thought-provoking
view of the West from which, despite (or perhaps because of?) its
common-sensical rationality, we can all learn.

NOTES

1. '*Stolitsa nashei "nerodiny" gorod-geroi Vashington Di. Si.*' – see, for
   example Vasilii Aksenov, 'Obzhivaia zapad', *Novyi amerikanets*,
   CLXXXIV (1983) (hereafter 'Oz'), p. 10.
2. 'Luchshee sostoianie literatury – emigratsiia', *Sem' dnei*, 50, 1984,
   pp. 21–4.
3. 'Obzhivaia zapad' – see note 1.
4. *V poiskakh grustnogo bebi* (New York, 1987) (hereafter *Vpgb*), p. 193.
5. *Vpgb*, 6. Aleksandr Zinov'ev described his situation rather more dra-
   matically: 'Emigration is for the Soviet writer just a protracted torture
   and, in the last analysis, execution': 'Rai i ad russkoi literatury', in
   'Kontinent kul'tury v Milane', *Tret'ia volna*, XV (1983) (hereafter
   'Riarl'), p. 47.
6. 'V avangarde – bez tylov', *Obozrenie*, XV (1985), p. 5.
7. These examples are taken from *Zolotaia nasha zhelezka* (Ann Arbor,
   Michigan, 1980) (hereafter *Znzh*), p. 140.
8. On this topic see P. Meyer, 'Basketball, God and the Ringo Kid:
   Philistinism and the Ideal in Aksënov's Short Stories', in E. Możejko
   et al. (eds) *Vasiliy Pavlovich Aksënov: A Writer in Quest of Himself*
   (Columbus, Ohio, 1986) (hereafter Możejko), pp. 119–30.
9. *Skazhi izium* (Ann Arbor, Michigan, 1985) (hereafter *Si*), p. 116.
10. It may be noted that Aksenov's avant-garde works were influenced by
    pre-revolutionary Russian writers rather than those of the American
    beat generation. See *Vpgb*, 300–31.
11. This is something of a regular theme in Aksenov's writing. See
    I. Lauridsen, 'Beautiful Ladies in the Works of Vasiliy Aksënov', in
    Możejko, pp. 102–18.
12. *Ozhog* (Ann Arbor, Michigan, 1980), p. 225.
13. *Ostrov Krym* (Ann Arbor, Michigan, 1980), p. 56.
14. In *Vpgb* (p. 86) Aksenov quotes Viktor Nekrasov's sovereign antidote to
    nostalgia – reading *Pravda*.
15. *Bumazhnyi peizazh* (Ann Arbor, Michigan, 1983) (hereafter *Bp*),
    p. 166.
16. A. Batchan and N. Sharymova, 'Prikliucheniia russkikh za granitsei.
    Beseda s Vasiliem Aksenovym', *Sem' dnei*, 13, 1984, (hereafter 'Prg'), 9.

17. Vasilii Aksenov, 'Ptichii bazar na Mankhettene', *Russkaia mysl'*, 28 February 1986, p. 6.
18. See, for example, 'Londonskii dnevnik', *Russkaia mysl'*, 2 May 1985, pp. 17–18.
19. Like several other expatriated Russian writers, including particularly Zinovii Zinik, Aksenov enjoys word play. One of his most felicitous coinings is the semi-Freudian '*odnobedrennaia kvartira*' (literally 'one-thighed flat') for 'one-bedroomed flat' – *Bp*, 158.
20. Very similar ideas are expressed in *Si*, 187.
21. Zinov'ev has declared, for instance, that 'the only reader adequate to high-quality Russian literature has remained in Russia': 'Riarl', 46.
22. In *Znzh* (p. 12) he refers ironically to 'our thoughtful, perceptive, well-disposed reader who is in our country, as everyone knows, the best in the world because he reads a lot in the metro'.
23. See 'Prg', 12.
24. 'Writers in Exile II: A Conference of Soviet and East European Dissidents', *Partisan Review*, 1, 1984, p. 32.
25. See, for example, Daniil Kharms, 'O iavleniiakh i sushchestvovaniakh No. 2', in his *Polet v nebesa* (Leningrad, 1988) p. 317.
26. See, for example, *Vpgb*, 253.
27. See 'Oz', 11.

7 Eduard Limonov and the Benefit of the Doubt

Robert Porter

Two recent weighty tomes on Russian literature published in the West – Victor Terras's *Handbook of Russian Literature* (Yale, 1985) and Wolfgang Kasack's *Entsiklopedicheskii slovar' russkoi literatury s 1917 goda* (London, 1988) – make no mention of Limonov. His first novel, *Eto ia – Edichka*, caused a scandal when it appeared in 1979. It is not the prime purpose of this article to add to the wide and at times intemperate debate about the book, but it may be as well to recall some of the reactions at the time: total condemnation, as in 'pro-Soviet pornography' (Gleizer, *Russkaia mysl'*), and 'a hollow man, writhing in semi-Trotskyist ravings' (Perel'man, *Novoe russkoe slovo)*, or unbridled enthusiasm: 'A novel-confession, splendid in its authenticity and warmth' (Sapgir, Moscow).[1] George Gibian offered a more middle-of-the road assessment: '"A good read", albeit far below the literary qualities of an Orwell or a Genet',[2] whilst the Soviet response at the time was predictable enough in its condemnation: Limonov typified the depths to which émigré writers could sink.[3] Since the advent of *glasnost'*, however, there has been more sympathetic coverage of Limonov in the Soviet press and even the prospect of publication of some of his works.[4] In between the neglect by the worthy compilers and surveyors of Russian literature on the one hand, and the passion expressed by reviewers on the other, there have been a number of learned articles indicating the literary tradition to which Limonov is heir and going some way to explaining the furore that the novel aroused. Titunik has produced an engaging discussion of the book in which he draws parallels with the eighteenth-century writer Vasilii Trediakovskii.[5] Ostracism and exile are at the back of such writing, and here Ovid and Catullus also find their place. Ann Shukman wrote an article which demonstrated, rather than merely proclaimed, the human qualities of Eddy: 'Behind the dandy and the nihilist and the sexual experimenter is the tender and hurt Edik Limonov who believes that love is the most important thing in the world',[6] and, she continues, 'at least we have to do here with a self that has some constancy and continuity behind the role-

62

playing, the acting and the narrating voices, a self in fact that confronts the alien and to some extent copes with the loneliness and deprivation which that entails' (Shukman, 13). Patricia Carden has written on Limonov's 'coming out' – both in the political and sexual sense.[7] Olga Matich has argued incisively for Limonov as a 'moral immoralist'.[8] She sees him as 'a literary provocateur'. . . . an unceremonious taboo breaker (Matich, 526). He also 'makes use of conflicting voices, ranging from outright provocation to a plea for the reader's love and acceptance. *Éto ja – Édička* features the gamut of the author's voices, whose dialogic or polyphonic chorus helps us to see the deeply "moral" nature of his "immoral hero"' (Matich, 537).

Since *Eto ia – Edichka*, Limonov has published two collections of poetry, four more novels, a collection of what might be termed prose poems and a number of short stories, yet there has been little discussion of these. If we are to examine the author's perceptions of the West, we can largely discount his works set in Kharkov, to wit *Podrostok Savenko* (Paris, 1983) and *Molodoi negodiai* (Paris, 1986). In so far as these works comment at all on the West, they do so on the basis of supposition. *Eto ia – Edichka, Dnevnik neudachnika* (New York, 1982), *Palach* (Jerusalem, 1986) and *L'Histoire de son serviteur* (Paris, 1984) at least purport to be based on first hand observation and experience. The last of these three has yet to appear in Russian, so it is fitting that for the time being we should concentrate on *Dnevnik neudachnika* and *Palach*.

The former is a seemingly random collection of thoughts and impressions, retaining the essential diary form that was one of the features of Limonov's first novel, yet being almost totally devoid of a story line, this book suggests something of a new departure. At the same time it sets out the chief characteristics of Limonov's attitudes to the West as they fully unfold in his other fiction.

First there is New York itself – filthy, sprawling, cluttered with garbage both literal and figurative. The observer of it fits in; he knows the geography well and can be just as violent and sordid as his setting. On at least two occasions in the book the city takes on a wholly grotesque aspect. For example, when his wife leaves him (that 'heavenly-hellish time'):

The time of the bared heart! Of strange air burning like alcohol, of monsters roaring all around, of a general conspiracy of nature against me, of fire-breathing sky, gaping and anxiously awaiting me.

How many improbable observations, how many nightmarish experiences! Through New York in the burning winter wind sabre-toothed tigers and other ice-age beasts prowled, the heavens burst open, and I, warm, damp and small, could scarcely leap away in time from the teeth, bellies and claws. A little bundle oozing blood.[9]

Very near the end of the book the hero has a job as a navvy, and almost each day he and his workmates find dead animals in the pit they are digging:

Our hole is very big. We have cleaned and swept our hole, prepared it like a bride. 'Our hole is a bride' – that is how I put it to the lads. The homosexual Carl said that that was a brilliant metaphor.

I stand in the hole and drink the coffee which Carl has given me. The hole is like a pregnant bride. There is a rock face as well in the hole – as white as a belly.

As white and as brown as a belly. (*Dnevnik neudachnika*, 241)

As with all of Limonov's stories set in New York, there is a precision about naming streets, districts and sleazy hotels, but the poet's eye frequently disorientates the reader. The narrator is childlike in many ways, but not least in his seemingly unpractised and 'new' ways of looking at the world. This is at a basic level not so dissimilar from the approach adopted by the Acmeists, and it is ironic that Limonov and his fellow poets who formed the group known as 'Concrete' in Moscow in 1971 rejected both Acmeists and Symbolists.[10]

Limonov's first novel shocked because of its sexual explicitness, or more precisely, its explicit depiction of homosexuality. Its shattering of linguistic taboos also outraged many – not just the use of the full range of Russian obscenities, but the manner in which it mixed various linguistic registers, imported wholesale foreign words, terminology and idiom. Curiously, the work's casual and repeated featuring of alcohol and hard-drug abuse aroused little comment, which leaves one to speculate as to the right-headedness of the righteous indignation that the novel's detractors expressed. In her reasoned response to the novel Ann Shukman wrote: 'By Western standards, however, *Edichka* has a curious innocence: it is quite without sadism for one thing. There is no rape, no sexual violence . . .' (Shukman, 2). *Dnevnik neudachnika* is likewise sexually explicit, but here we have elements of the sado-masochism that is to become the main theme in *Palach*. With his girlfriend 'the bald singer' the hero attends an induction session – sadism this time; masochism is promised for another occasion. The narrator's bisexuality is also on display.

Running counter to all the spiritual and physical squalor in *Dnevnik neudachnika*, there is one persistent image: flowers, and all their associations. To take one random example: 'Wild flowers burst into colour on both sides of the road, and where it changed direction the low sea glittered, and life was like revolver fire, like random and sinister revolver fire' (p. 70). Occasionally the flower imagery links up with reminiscences of his former life in Russia, but, as always with Limonov, the tiny pockets of sentimentality are quickly blasted away. One entry, pointedly entitled 'Pastoral' (p. 82) is set in East Germany (midway, so to speak, between Russia and the West), yet the fairly sustained picture of peace and rural tranquility ends with the suicide of two young people.

The political nihilism which is so prevalent in Limonov's first novel is also to be found in *Dnevnik neudachnika*. The narrator prefers small circulation extremist newspapers. He repeatedly imagines himself to be a revolutionary hero like Che Guevera: he relishes equally the power and the unbridled violence of the mob. However, at times he pictures himself on the mausoleum in Moscow, an established political leader, but he is also 'the little poet' (*poetik*) who will overturn the government for a huge sum of money. He seems unable to resolve the twin urges within himself to be a national or international hero on the one hand, and the rebellious individual who rejects anything that is already established on the other. As the work progresses, one can see that the hero's roots are to be found not in twentieth-century ideology, but in Dostoevskii's Underground Man. One suspects that Limonov has too much respect for his literary ancestor to mention him directly here – in any case *Dnevnik neudachnika*, like most of Limonov's works, abounds in literary references generally, but in this instance the author alludes to Chekhov and O'Neil; and then, as he recounts his various menial jobs, he loses the one thing that is most precious to him, his identity: 'I, we, usually come in "through the side door", down the back stairs. Our place is the servants' quarters or the basement, where we stoke the boilers, do the laundry and the ironing and so on' (p. 239). A little later he announces that he will go underground (*podpol'e*) and declare war on everyone (p. 248).

There is an illuminating phrase in Limonov's own description of his stylistic method, which glosses precisely the sentiments quoted above:

> Limonov's poetic style . . . is characterised by the widespread use of the primitive, of convention (*primitiv, uslovnost'*). One can also speak of 'Limonov's bureaucratic-Dostoevskian lexicon' (*o chinovnich'e-dostoevskoi leksike Limonova*). (*Apollon*, 43–6)

Thus it can be argued that the main thrust of the work is the struggle for identity in the bewildering world of emigration. The hero is reduced to the state of childlike defiance, alternating with wild enthusiasm and a thirst for adventure. The author tries on various personalities and never hesitates to inform us of his current employment or station in life: 'I am also a cleaning-man, I can also be called a vacuum-man . . . I am also a floor scrubber . . . and five days a week I am a navvy, a bricklayer and a carpenter . . .' (*Dnevnik neudachnika*, 239).

Palach is a different story from the non-sadistic, non-violent *Eto ia – Edichka*. The work is just as explicit as the author's first novel, but the subject matter this time is sado-masochism. Thus one is led to revise the view of *Eto ia – Edichka* as a straight confession. It would seem that Limonov is keen to flout all sexual proprieties, and, one might argue, the author challenges all accepted values – sexual, political, linguistic. Indeed, it would not be going too far to say that Limonov also challenges accepted Western pornographic values. In the discussion surrounding *Eto ia – Edichka* allusion was sometimes made to the notorious French classic *L'Histoire d'O*, by the pseudonymous Pauline Réage, a sexual fantasy utterly devoid of comedy. Eddy has only scorn for the film based on this novel and for similar offerings (*'poshlosti'*, *'sladkie seksual'nye siropy'*: p. 132), which he feels have sent his wife off her head. Eddy's world is one of enforced squalor, poverty and struggle. By contrast O, living in utter luxury, actively chooses punishment, torture, humiliation and, ultimately, death. In *Palach* it is as if Limonov is defiantly declaring to the West that if it wants pornography, then it shall have it, but only on Limonov's terms, that is, with a good deal of disdain and professed tedium. The hero, Oscar Khudzinski, a Polish émigré in New York, gets a phone call from his girlfriend, Natasha, a Russian:

> 'Come over right away and fuck me till my eyes pop out of my head, eh?' whispered Natasha, breathing deeply and quickly, knowing perfectly well what effect this special whisper of hers had on Oscar.
> Offended, Oscar said nothing.
> 'O, take a taxi and come over. Right away, I've really got the hots lying here, and I can't keep my legs still . . .'
> 'Oh', Oscar sighed at last into the receiver, 'You're a real tart, aren't you, Natal'ia?'
> The tart giggled down the phone.
> 'Come over', she said again, quickly, 'And you know what, please bring the whip and that big rubber member of yours. I want you to rape me and beat me, and afterwards to fuck me with that huge rubber member'. Natasha sighed and stopped . . .
> 'Okay, I'll come right away', Oscar agreed dejectedly, and hung up. (*Palach*, 13)

Oscar's reaction here seems to bear out the sentiments expressed in a recent book about the pornography trade, co-authored by that lapsed Slavist Nick Anning:

> We found the pornography trade a complex and challenging subject, though there were times when we were revolted by the more extreme material, especially that depicting sex with children. As for enjoying research on the products, we are the living refutation that pornography is addictive: boring is a more appropriate adjective.[11]

So what are Oscar's perceptions of the West? They can be considered under three headings: career and material well-being, the hero's images of himself in the West, and moral attitudes.

Firstly then, like Eddy, Oscar is torn between the spiritual and the material. Unlike Eddy, he makes good financially, but his anguish, like Eddy's, remains. Other Poles have made successful careers in emigration – Roman Polanski, Jerzy Kosinski, the Pope. Other émigrés from Eastern Europe have also done well, the Czech Miloš Forman, or the Russians Nuriev and Baryshnikov (pp. 23–4). So why should not this thirty-six-year-old émigré of six years' standing? Having witnessed a killing in a hamburger joint the hero is prompted, on reading that the victim was a 'professional sadist', to make his own way in the world by the same means. He quickly acquires a number of wealthy middle-aged female clients. A millionairess Gabrielle Kroniadis, who among other things enjoys being dressed up as a schoolgirl, scolded and mercilessly spanked, sets him up in a luxury apartment.

Very quickly Oscar turns into a snob – he shuns his old down-and-out friends, and resents the vulgarity of his Russian girlfriend, and especially the men she still cultivates, notably Charlie, a six-foot-six forty-year-old transvestite, who uses the name Dolores at the hero's birthday party (p. 164). In stark contrast to Eddy, Oscar has all that money can buy. Career and well-being also bestow on him a sense of identity and belonging: 'I am a torturer, that is, a professional sadist . . . Geneviève is embarrassed by my profession, but I'm not, not at all. I'm even proud of it . . .' (p. 118), he willingly explains to the writer Steve Baron. This certainty is in clear opposition to the various occupations that the narrator of *Dnevnik neudachnika* desperately lays claim to in his searching for a role and an identity.

Charlie's transvestitism is mirrored in a sense by the uncertain status and role of Oscar's fellow-countryman Jacek Gutor. He once took Oscar in for a few weeks and fed him while he was out of work. While Gabrielle is intrigued by him, Oscar dismisses him as a madman, but in doing so indicates the anomalous situation of the émigré that we know only too well from Limonov's other books:

> Once I had to live at his place for a few weeks. While I was there he was mugging up 'The History of Philosophy' one volume after another . . . What normal man would in our time study Confucius or Lao-tzu in Polish, in New York? (p. 166)

Oscar embarked on his lucrative career because of a murder. At the end of the story he himself is murdered, probably by Jacek. The clue is in the strange question that Jacek asks Gabrielle: 'Could you kiss a cockroach?' and which comes to epitomise for some of the characters Jacek's bizarre nature. He lives alone, he shuns sex, he is surrounded by old Polish books. He is outraged by the orgy at Oscar's birthday party, and feels that America corrupts. The area of New York he now inhabits reminds Oscar of Poland (p. 196). This 'God's fool', as he is referred to at one point (p. 179), makes quite an impression on the women at Oscar's party, and it is Natasha who suggests the reason: 'only a madman could today, now, in our age, preach not hatred, which we all carry within us, but love. Love, Oscar . . .' (p. 206). Jacek advocates love even towards hideous insects, and he objects to Oscar's sadistic dealings with Gabrielle. At the end of the story, after receiving several death threats, Oscar is stabbed to death and a dead cockroach is found in his mouth.

Jacek and Oscar can be taken to represent the two possible resolutions of the riven personality that was Eddy and the narrator of *Dnevnik neudachnika*. Oscar embraces the American way of life and his problems of identity disappear – he becomes one of the celebrities whose names are so liberally sprinkled throughout the text, and New York becomes his city (p. 156), and all its women belong to him, so far as he is concerned. The death threats that are made against him he is more than willing to put down to his new-found fame. After the feature in the pornographic magazine *Real Man*, he is sure some unhinged admirer is trying to oust him, some 'double', in just the same way as John Lennon was murdered by someone who wanted to be like him.

At the outset of the story we are told of Oscar's theory concerning the dominant intelligentsia. Since coming to America, the hero has been planning a socio-philosophical book, but so far has not got beyond some provisional notes. He classes Caesar and Hitler as intellectuals, but would like to find a new term for 'intelligentsia':

In his book Oscar had also done away with the class theory. Oscar maintained that there were only two biological classes existing in the world: 5 per cent were active people, leaders, those whom Oscar called approximately 'intellectuals', or sometimes 'the dominant ones', and 95 per cent were all the rest, the masses. Oscar had taken the statistics from the latest biological research. (p. 27)

There are no prizes for suggesting the likely source for this notion, and, indeed, it is best understood as one of many allusions to all manner of literary giants which Oscar makes, the better to satisfy his own ego. However, it is significant that he moves from a position of quiet disdain for popular literature (the scene where he subjugates Susan Woodyard, the authoress of titillating fiction, must rank as one of the most explicit in the book, or witness the assessment of Steve Baron's blockbuster *Elena's Choice*, full of 'pseudo-humanitarian argumentation and truths that everyone knows already': p. 117) to a situation where he is very much part of pulp culture. Steve Baron becomes a close friend. Oscar's conscience does not suffer when he takes his whip to his victims, but his self does.

Secondly, Oscar's self is made up of three elements: his past life in Poland, now only dimly glimpsed; his contemplation of his own image now he is an émigré; and his attempt at rebirth. He recalls his girlfriend Elżbieta, and how he made love to her on Easter day, 'the sacred day of his devout parents' (p. 12). He hates talking about politics, for it is conducted in the clichés of Western commentators. He left Poland, he tells us, for personal reasons (p. 68). When, in a fit of jealousy, he breaks into Natasha's flat he discovers a letter from her parents whom she has clearly misled about her occupation in the West (p. 112). The episode points up the rootlessness of émigrés, yet the old life cannot be dismissed. Lying in bed of a morning Oscar is often assailed by thoughts of his childhood, his parents and insignificant vignettes of his existence in a small Polish provincial town; as he tells himself: 'the whole of life consists only of episodes like these' (p. 97). After his birthday party which is supposedly to mark his re-birth, he breaks with Gabrielle, and for the first time in a long while prepares himself some soup, an enactment of the advice his mother gave him years before, and a living reminder that, try as he might, he cannot escape from himself (pp. 97 and 231).

He is occasionally billed as a philosopher or writer in polite company, for he studied in the philosophical faculty at Warsaw University, but his studies hang as suspended as Raskol'nikov's, and he is anxious to proclaim his real profession. He frequently questions his own identity, staring in the mirror and forcing comparisons. He decides he does not look like a philosopher (p. 57), and does his hair like the early Elvis Presley. He imagines himself ranking with all manner of celebrities, including Mick Jagger (p. 83), and he wants Andy Warhol to come to his party (p. 140). As he contemplates himself in his huge mirror, he comes to think of himself in the third person. Conducting an imaginary conversation with Andy Warhol, he asserts that he has created a new form of existence in capitalist society, a new form of art. Within the narrative framework of the novel, this scene is not entirely fanciful, for Oscar has seen Warhol more than once socially and spoken to him.

Oscar's narcissism is, of course, a common trait in Limonov's heroes, but it is not exclusive. Vanity is presented as just another human indulgence. Unlike Narcissus, Oscar does not spend all his time contemplating himself, but his death is brought about largely by his own self-regard. His extravagant birthday party features a surprise corpse called 'Arthur' around whom the revellers are to cavort. The unworldly Jacek Gutor finds this all too much and it precipitates him towards homicide. Rebirth turns out to be death.

Thirdly, regarding the perceptions of the West, we have the moral aspect. As with *Eto ia – Edichka*, it appears almost out of place to discuss the moral attitudes displayed in a work that at first sight seems to be so thoroughly tasteless. Sadism, masochism, homosexuality, followed by hints of necrophilia, incest, and child abuse (Oscar's bride-to-be had dealings with her father when she was twelve years old) all find a place in *Palach*. Indeed, the only sexual perversion not to figure would seem to be sex with an animal – for that one has to go to *Dnevnik neudachnika* where the narrator at one point tries to persuade a dog to bestow certain favours on him (p. 108).

Yet there is a kind of moral awareness in the novel. To start with, Oscar is not his creator, and such a division between author and hero is not as pronounced in Limonov's other works. Moreover, despite all his desires to succeed in the environment in which he finds himself, the hero hates his surroundings. *Palach* is perhaps better understood not just as a Russian novel, but also as a novel of New York. The neuroses, the squalor, the sexual uninhibitedness, the violence, the mutual exclusivity of material well-being and spiritual worth, the attempts at establishing an identity and at finding acceptance, and, above all, the confusion experienced by the individual – all these have been well chronicled in novels like Philip Roth's *Portnoy's Complaint* through to Tama Janowitz's *Slaves of New York* and *A Cannibal in Manhattan*. Of *Portnoy's Complaint* Tony Tanner writes:

> All doors on all the rooms of his childhood are opened and while this permits us to see the comic-desperate strategies of the sexually maturing child, it also enables us to hear the cacophony of conflicting imperatives which beset him, and to become aware of the irrational rules and emotional bullyings which were visited on the bewildered child. It is in this way that self-obsession merges with social observation . . .[12]

Is not Portnoy's Jewish upbringing Limonov's Soviet State?
And Roth himself wrote:

> The American writer in the middle of the twentieth century has his
> hands full in trying to describe, and then to make *credible*, much of
> the American reality. It stupifies, it sickens, it infuriates, and
> finally, it is even a kind of embarrassment to one's own meagre
> imagination. The actuality is continually outdoing our talents, and
> the culture tosses up figures almost daily that are the envy of any
> novelist.[13]

Forced to take the subway at three o'clock in the morning, Oscar is
revolted by the smell of urine, the filth and the intimidation he feels
when confronted by half a dozen hooligans. His thoughts are driven
back to Poland. He asks himself if he is a racist. He is especially
struck by the graffiti he sees: 'I fuck the world'. Yet there are
manifold ironies in the situation, for he subscribes to the sentiment of
the graffiti, and he sees himself as being outside the racial conflict –
they can cut each others' throats, and he will clear off to Europe with
his Natasha (p. 86). A little later he concludes that New Yorkers
must be masochists to walk the dirtiest streets in the world. He is
reminded of a Baltic village he once visited where pedigree dogs
interbred with the local mongrels and an extraordinary mixed canine
race flourished. The population of New York seems no different to
him:

> The population of New York, mused Oscar as he strode east along
> Bleecker Street, was not behind the canine population of that
> village when it came to absurdity and outlandishness. The mix of
> races and tribes, though sometimes successful, more often than not
> had produced the weirdest of specimens, a parade of monsters and
> ominous clowns passed before Oscar's eyes. Some of the creatures
> did not even resemble people, but reminded you more of objects.
> Look at this man in the huge trousers leaning against the post-box,
> a hideous bubble of dropsy, not a person. Someone had torn half
> the face off the old man in the dirty checkered jacket. The lad with
> the watery eyes did not even have a suggestion of a chin. Mutants.
> People of the future. (p. 89)

At one point after the party Oscar refers to New York as Baghdad,
where 'everything is possible' (p. 187). Baghdad is, of course, noted

in fiction for its magic, but also for its juxtaposition of opulence and poverty, as well as for its tyrants and its rags-to-riches fairy-tales. On one level Oscar is a tyrant to certain willing victims, and his is indeed a story of rags to riches. But he comes to resent his reliance on Gabrielle, and there are authorial hints that in fact Oscar is enslaved by his apparent dominant position. The scene we have already noted where the hero claims New York as his own, closes as follows:

> The wind of New York, strong and fresh, flew in through the window, amiably licked Oscar's lips, an ample gust caressed his face and blew throughout the penthouse, touching the walls and the flowers like the master of the house (*po-khoziaiski*). (p. 156)

Oscar is thus seduced, possessed by the big city and all that it stands for, and not the other way round. Limonov takes his hero out of the gutter, builds him up, ensnares him and kills him off, reserving the last laugh for himself, his readers, and for the eccentric Jacek Gutor, who urges all to love, to love even cockroaches. In this resides the morality of *Palach*.

The work frequently referred to in *Eto ia – Edichka* which Limonov published in *Apollon* (p. 57–62), 'My – natsional'nyi geroi', is a mixture of autobiography and fantasy, and as such should be treated with some caution. None the less, it does serve as a useful key to the author's longer prose. Dated May 1974, Moscow, the piece tells how Limonov and his wife Elena Shchapova arrive in Paris at the personal invitation of the French President. They are made honorary citizens of France. Limonov is to be in a film directed by Antonioni, and is soon invited out to a restaurant by Salvador Dali. Dali illustrates Limonov's books of verse and Limonov makes Dali some unusual old-fashioned trousers. It would seem safe to assume that this is on the whole fantasy, as is the author's account of some of his exploits in Russia – for example, playing Razin, Pugachev, Chapaev, Esenin and himself in various films. Yet these statements illustrate that Limonov enjoys wearing his vanities up front and that he relishes the role of violent revolutionary folk-hero and poet. He claims to have taken Elena away from her rich husband, while he himself was poor. In seven years in Moscow he had 126 different rooms and flats. The first American hippies made their appearance, the author tells us, in

1967, but he had been sleeping rough since 1960. These 'facts' tell us about Limonov's psychology, if nothing else. He claims that the greatest influence on him was a workmate in a factory with whom he read Kafka in Ukrainian translation. He repeatedly asserts that he epitomises the Russian people. He was the son of a junior officer in the Soviet army. He tells us: 'All my life has been a struggle against generally accepted morality'. He insists that unlike Esenin in America and Blok in Paris, he does not see just chaos; he looks closely at the problems of France and the West in general. He also reminds us that a government minister gave 'the first Russian poet Trediakovskii' a beating with a stick (*Apollon*, 60).

How appropriate that in this comic, ebullient and conceited testimony, Limonov should allude to Salvador Dali, for the Spanish painter in his autobiography and in his paintings presented the public with a dilemma not so dissimilar to that posed by Limonov. In his famous essay on Dali, Orwell conceded that Dali was technically very talented, but expressed his abhorence of the necrophilia, masturbation, sadism and narcissism in which he revelled. He argues that we have in Dali 'a direct, unmistakable assault on sanity and decency'.[14] He denies Dali any 'benefit of clergy' that others might wish to extend to him on the grounds of his artistry, and concludes that 'such pictures as "Mannequin rotting in a taxi-cab" . . . are diseased and disgusting, and any investigation ought to start out from that fact' (p. 262).

The foregoing discussion of some of Limonov's works has not proceeded in the fashion Orwell suggested for Dali. For one thing, the sexual revolution that has taken place in Western literature since the War makes it difficult to see Limonov's writing as primarily an assault on sanity and decency. Rather, our comments have taken as their principle the advice that Orwell offers elsewhere in his essay – namely that 'it is doubtful policy to suppress anything' (p. 259), or by the same token, to pretend that it does not exist. Can we not give Limonov, if not benefit of clergy, then at least the benefit of the doubt, and accept at face value his assertion that all his life he has struggled against 'generally accepted morality'? Limonov's heroes are sinned against as much as they are sinners, and the world in which they find themselves oppresses as much as it liberates. It is therefore not such a bad thing to challenge the morality of that world. Limonov's irreverence – even for our own well-established values in what might be termed 'popular adult fiction' – has a certain justification.

NOTES

1. Much of this comment is reproduced in the frontispiece to the novel: E. Limonov, *Eto ia – Edichka* (New York, 1979).
2. G. Gibian, '"Russianness" and Twentieth-Century Emigres', in O. Matich (ed.), *The Third Wave: Russian Literature in Emigration* (Ann Arbor, Michigan, 1984) (hereafter *The Third Wave*), p. 77.
3. L. Pochivalov, 'Chelovek na dne', *Literaturnaia gazeta*, 10 September 1980.
4. D. Iakushkin, 'Eto on, Edichka' (interview), *Moskovskie novosti*, 32, 6 August 1989, p. 16.
5. I. Titunik, 'Vasilii Trediakovskii and Eduard Limonov: Erotic Reverberations in the History of Russian Literature', in N. Brostrom ed., *Papers in Slavic Philology*, IV (Ann Arbor, Michigan, 1984), pp. 393–404.
6. A. Shukman, 'Taboos, Splits and Signifiers: Limonov's *Eto ya – Edichka*', *Essays in Poetics*, VIII, 2 (1983), pp. 1–18.
7. P. Carden, 'Limonov's Coming Out', in *The Third Wave*, pp. 221–9.
8. O. Matich, 'The Moral Immoralist: Edward Limonov's *Eto ja – Edička*', *Slavic and East European Journal*, XXX, 4 (1986) (hereafter Matich), pp. 526–40.
9. *Dnevnik neudachnika*, p. 145.
10. E. Limonov, 'Poety gruppy "Konkret"' and 'My – natsional'nyi geroi', both in M. Shemiakin (ed.), *Apollon 77* (Paris, 1977) (hereafter *Apollon*), pp. 43–6 and 57–62 respectively.
11. D. Hebditch and N. Anning, *Porn Gold* (London, 1988), p. xi.
12. T. Tanner, *City of Words: American Fiction 1950–1970* (London, 1971), p. 313.
13. Quoted in A. Kazin, *Bright Book of Life: American Storytellers from Hemingway to Mailer* (London, 1974), p. 147.
14. G. Orwell, *The Penguin Essays of George Orwell* (Harmondsworth, 1984), p. 257.

8 The West, and in particular France, through the Eyes of a Distracted Russian
Anatolii Gladilin

'I knew my beloved by his walk . . .'. I do not know about anyone else, but I came across this song for the first time as performed by Alesha Dmitrievich on tapes brought to me from Paris in the early 1960s. But I should like to start elsewhere. Twenty years later and already a well-established émigré, I was taking a walk through New York. I love walking. I have always liked Manhattan and on this occasion I had decided to walk down to the bay from the Fifties. That is about 100 blocks, no great distance for me. In Lower Manhattan strict geometry blurs, the streets begin to curve and meander, and at one point I thought I had lost my way. Wall Street ought to have been nearby, but where precisely? I wanted to watch the sharks of imperialism teeming in their skyscrapers. I knew that I would not be allowed into the banks to see how they made their money, but I just wanted to walk past and imbibe the air of profit. When wandering about an unfamiliar city you have to ask passers-by the way. I could ask in English 'How do I get to Wall Street?'. Understanding the answer was quite another matter. But then they would probably point me in the right direction, and I could work it out from there myself . . .

I turned to a pair of lads grilling kebabs on the kerbside. Lunchtime was approaching and the streets were clearly filling with vendors of hot snacks and cool drinks. By the way, only a Soviet could imagine that all Americans live it up in restaurants and bars in their lunchbreak. Nowadays office workers prefer a hot snack on the street, something cheap if less than cheerful.

And so I approached the two kebab-vendors, who were of course not dressed in the regulation suit and tie of all shop-assistants, and so could not be distinguished from the New York crowd. One last step, then something inside me clicked. I swallowed my prepared English

76

phrase and asked them in Russian, 'How do I get to Wall Street, lads?'. I thought that if I were met with incomprehension, I would apologise and repeat the question in English. But the lads, who had also been watching me for a few seconds, spying a potential customer, blithely answered in pure Russian, 'Straight ahead then turn that way', and one added, 'Perhaps you want Number Sixteen?'. I answered no, thanked them, and tramped on.

Now think for a moment; beyond an ocean, a continent away from the Motherland, not somewhere in Brighton Beach, but in the respectable quarters where world capital holds court, I unerringly found my compatriots. Moreover, they were not surprised. In other words, they spotted me in the crowd. And to think that I took myself to be a solid Westerner. 'I knew my beloved by his walk . . .'.

I must add that it is still a mystery why he asked me about 'Number Sixteen'. I would very much doubt that there is a shelter for homeless Russians in some building on Wall Street.

And so, beyond seas and oceans, we still recognise each other, as in the neat squares of Old Europe. You cannot tell immediately whether he is Soviet or a local, where he popped up from in order to see the Sistine Madonna in the Louvre, whether from Cheliabinsk or Jerusalem, from Detroit or Barnaul, but you can sense that he is Russian, or at least from the Soviet Union, before he even opens his mouth.

Of course, there are times when you are left in no doubt. A good friend of ours, Russian, naturally, recounted the following incident: she was taking a group of American tourists around four European capitals. (The group was made up of Soviet Jewish émigrés who had made a good living in the States and now wanted, as good Americans, to travel in comfort around the old Continent, to inflict their own particular revenge for hungry and downtrodden Ladispolis and Ostia.) And so they went to visit an exhibition, or rather a sale of diamonds in Amsterdam. The wily Dutch salesman spotted immediately those who might be interested in diamonds and praised his wares to the skies, while not taking his eyes off an elderly Jewish lady from, you guessed it, Brighton Beach. The lady could not stand the pressure. Her eyes gleamed. 'Cover me', she asked our friend, unbuttoning her blouse and pulling out of her bra with the usual gesture of a Kharkov market trader a crumpled wad of 2,000 dollars.

If some highly-placed comrade from the Soviet Embassy is reading this at the moment, I can almost see the ironic, supercilious smile on his well-fed face; there you have it, these wretched émigrés have blundered into Europe to be fleeced. . . . Fine. So here is another example. If I may, I should like to quote extensively from the travelogue 'A Cultural Crusade to Vaux-le-Vicomte', contained in a book of my essays and articles, published in 1980 under the general title of *Parizhskaia iarmarka*. This book swiftly vanished from the bookstalls, and I do not think that it is available anymore. I am ready to bet that no-one at this conference knows the text.

And so my wife, daughter and I were visiting the chateau of Vaux-le-Vicomte, 50 km from Paris, and I went off to wander through the avenues of the park. I quote:

Suddenly from around the corner came two men, in no way remarkable in appearance. But, I swear, they caught my eye at once. An expression of desperate longing passed over the faces of these strangers – much in the way that Moscow alcoholics, longing for the hair of the dog, look at an off-licence before eleven o'clock strikes and you can buy a bottle of vodka. And they looked at me expectantly, as if I were a 'third man' with whom they could split the cost of a friendly bottle of vodka. But I dismissed these unconscious associations. No, I decided, this could not be, I was seeing things. After all, I was in France, not on Lenin Prospect. Then two youngish ladies entered the clearing, and once again I gasped. Imagine two Soviet shop-assistants from the vegetable counter draped in dazzling French clothes with hair dyed so bright that a driver would instinctively slam on his brakes. I thought I was dreaming again. Then one of the women asked the other, 'So why have Vovka and Lenka run on ahead?'.

All became clear. I turned back to the bench where my wife and daughter were waiting. On seeing me they pressed their fingers to their lips and my daughter whispered, 'Hush, don't speak Russian; it looks as though they're from the Embassy or Trade Mission'.

The participants in this official cultural crusade filed past us, suspecting nothing, loudly discussing official mundanities. I shall not go into the details of their conversations; let us not betray state secrets.

'Misha, off you go, your papa is waiting', called a woman nearby to a child collecting chestnuts, 'Misha, how long are you going to keep us waiting?'. My daughter could restrain herself no longer; 'Misha, listen to your mama', she said in Russian.

No doubt had masked bandits with revolvers burst out of the

bushes at that moment, they would not have produced such a startling effect. Seizing the child, the woman took to her heels, glancing back in fear.

An amusing occurrence, no doubt. But we returned to the car thinking the same thing: 'My God, what an unhappy nation we are. Why do fellow-countrymen, meeting far from home, fear even to strike up a conversation with each other?'

Of course this essay was written in the so-called 'Time of Stagnation'. In those days Soviet comrades were very frightened of meeting émigrés. Now it is a different matter. No doubt the aim, if not to widen contacts, is at least not to avoid them. None the less a friend from Radio Liberty recounted the following story recently. He was attending M.S. Gorbachev's press conference in Paris. After the press conference he bumped into a stranger in the corridor. They exchanged glances, smiled, and started speaking Russian. How they recognised each other will remain a mystery to Slavists. A second mystery, after that, of the Russian Soul.

'Who are you?', my friend asked the stranger. The latter identified himself. He turned out to be a journalist on a very bold progressive Moscow magazine. In turn my friend identified himself. At the words 'Radio Liberty' the Soviet correspondent jumped in fright, but then pulled himself together bravely and, glancing around, whispered, 'What do you think, is there a big KGB presence here?'.

I do not think that I am straying from the conference theme by talking about Soviet-émigré meetings. After all émigrés have become an essential and very intriguing aspect of Western life for Soviets. Soviet delegations, tours by Soviet theatres and musicians, the general interest in the Soviet Union, especially since the emergence of *perestroika* – these are all important elements in the new realities of émigré life. From the earlier part of my talk you now have an idea of how émigrés regard Soviet comrades, but how are émigrés seen in the eyes of Soviet people? . . .

Neglecting the old saw 'don't carve your thoughts in wood', I shall cite examples that only concern me. Oh yes, I had the honour of becoming a literary character in a Soviet novel. Not so long ago Iulian Semenov's novel *Auktsion* was printed in a run of many millions in the Soviet Union. I do not have this immortal oeuvre at hand and so cannot quote from it accurately, and shall therefore restrict myself to a paraphrase of one episode.

The Paris correspondent of Radio Liberty, a failed writer called Godilin (I think you know who the author means) arrived in London for the press conference of a respected antiquarian and friend of the USSR. At the press conference Godilin asked insinuating and provocative questions, at which point someone from the Soviet Embassy rose in anger and made for Godilin. At the sound of Russian speech Godilin fled headlong from the room, knocking over chairs as he ran . . .

Another example. The Leningrad author Viktor Konetskii published his foreign impressions last year in the magazine *Neva*. There, as it happens, Konetskii recalled how Anatolii Gladilin rang him in his Paris hotel room, how he, Konetskii, curtly and abruptly dealt with him, and how Gladilin, instead of hanging up, debased himself with flattery. At *Neva* they no doubt thought this story reliable, for they published it.

Auktsion is pre-perestroika literature, but Konetskii's essay was published at the very peak of perestroika – however, the picture is one and the same: bold Soviet chaps coolly rebuffing wretched émigré provocateurs.

In general, I knew my beloved by his walk . . .

Now to return to the main topic. Irrespective of 'sovietness' or 'unsovietness', irrespective of material and social position, what marks us out in the Western crowd? By what secret signs do we recognise each other? We are distinguished and united by one factor alone: Western life drives us to distraction.

I would even suggest that this distraction can be qualified. I first came to Paris in an official delegation of the Union of Soviet Writers at the age of twenty-five. This was my first and only trip to a capitalist country. In those days they gave us simply microscopic amounts of francs. You could not even consider dropping into a café for a cup of coffee. But I had absolutely no interest in either the luxurious shop-windows or the abundance of delicatessens; I could just wander for days around the city, admiring the architecture, following the stream of cars, watching the crowds milling on the pavements. Had I been offered the choice of a sumptious meal in Maxim's or another hour to while away on the grand boulevards in the rain – without even thinking I would have chosen the latter. To this day I cannot work out why Paris drove me to distraction – was it the violet twilight, the girls in mini-skirts, the easy-going people, the unfamiliar sense of freedom? Again I cannot say, but this was the Paris of my youth, and I shall never see its like again. When fifteen years later I arrived in Paris, as they say, for permanent residence, I saw that it was already quite a different city.

Last year, at a meeting of Soviet and émigré writers in the European Parliament building in Strasbourg, I spoke to a young official from the Soviet Embassy. Indeed, you could already feel different winds blowing, and the Soviet comrades were very polite and attentive to the émigrés. And so, I was telling the lad from the Embassy that Paris was, of course, wonderful for tourists, but its nervous rhythm wore out the Parisians themselves, it was simply a difficult city to live in. I sensed that the lad from the Embassy, who had been working in Paris for only a few months, did not understand me. No doubt he saw Paris through the romantic eyes of my youth.

And so, there is such a romantic madness.

I would suggest, however, that another form of distraction is more prevalent (I think you are used to my terminology) – everyday distraction. In Vienna, the first transit point for émigrés (I myself passed through Vienna and often travel there to meet friends) nobody at first pays any attention to the luxurious shop-windows. It is the food-shops that shock you. Food which in the Soviet Union you fought for, stood in endless queues for, seized in open combat, obtained by subscription or by influence is available here on a take-it-or-leave-it basis, and still shopkeepers press and badger you to buy. In shabby little Austria, defeated in the war, there are strawberries on the counters as early as May, and the variety of sausage and ham is unimaginable. This can be called 'consumer shock'. This same 'consumer shock' also affects the hordes of Soviet tourists who now wander around Western cities on invitations from their émigré relatives. But Soviets also feel deceived and degraded: all their lives they were forced to toil to overfulfil the plan, to sweat and labour, and in return were given a beggarly level of subsistence, whereas here in the West it seems as if grass springs from the very asphalt. It is true that after the initial shock Soviets develop an interest in cars and especially clothes and electro-technology, which can be taken back to the Soviet Union to pay for the cost of the trip. Moreover, so much has been written about consumer and material shock that I do not propose to discuss it any further.

The reaction of Soviets and émigrés to Western democracy and political institutions is much more curious. At once I exclude from consideration articles in the Soviet press from travellers recently returned from abroad, or papers given to European universities, where it is required to espouse views of the moderate left and not to express extreme opinions. To summarise, you find a remarkable unanimity in conference corridors, in the kitchens of émigré flats, in cafés, where disciplined members of the CPSU debate confidentially with those former 'leftists' and 'dissidents' who departed for the West to escape the partocracy's oppression. They all agree that the West doesn't know it's born. Why do they strike? Can anyone really be dissatisfied with such a way of life? The crime-rate? What crime-rate? It's just Arabs, Pakistanis, other blacks. They should have been sent back to Africa long ago to run around in their villages! Those feminists are just silly tarts. They should come to the Soviet Union and try working on the railway! Freedom of speech has addled their brains; why, they don't even respect their government! Mind you, they're not wrong; how can you respect such a government? Western presidents and ministers are just cowards; a couple of atom bombs would have taken care of Tehran and Tripoli long ago. . . . The figure they all find most sympathetic here, whether he be strong and sturdy or polite and elegant, depending on the given country, is that of the policeman. It would be splendid if they were licenced to shoot motorcyclists as well, as Vail' and Genis noted so acutely. . . . Are they really so hamstrung? . . . Or don't you know your beloved by his walk?

I have said this many times before, and shall do so again; irrespective of our political views, whether we live in the Soviet Union or the West, whether we have turned our backs on our country or rejoice at *perestroika*, all of us, I repeat, were, are and shall remain Soviet people, with the possible exceptions of Rostropovich and Aksenov. And Soviet Man, as soon as he has overcome the shock, wants as a first step to bring real order to the West. And he would do so if only you gave him the chance!

We welcome freedom of the press in the West heart and soul. We are convinced that the press should only print the truth. But we only accept the truth that suits and pleases us. If someone persists in holding different views, especially if they contradict ours, then they are obviously 'agents of the KGB' or the 'CIA', and generally sold their souls to the Bolsheviks or Japanese intelligence long ago. . . . Read the 'Editor's Column' in *Kontinent*, where you will find the firm stamp of *Pravda* from the days of Andrei Ianuar'evich Vyshinskii, unsullied by shades of dark or light. Nowadays *Pravda*, the organ of the Central Committee of the CPSU, is a pale imitation of the 'Editor's Column'. Moreover this is quite understandable, as they have *glasnost'* and *perestroika* in the Soviet Union these days. A different style is in fashion. You can hardly find those fondly-remembered and heart-warming Stalinist formulas in *Molodaia gvardiia* or *Nash sovremennik* any more. You may protest that I am taking extreme examples. But if anything has been achieved by *perestroika* in the Soviet Union, then it is freedom of speech: although not long ago the literary critic Alla Latynina appeared on Soviet Television in the programme 'Vzgliad'. She said how strange it was to hear unambiguous proposals in the speeches of respected liberal Soviet writers to put the opponents of *perestroika* 'up against the wall'.

I am not certain of the date, but I think that Soviet Man was born as a new type in 1918, when he wrapped his ardent heart in a leather jacket and started to reconstruct the world around him with pure hands and a clear head. Pay no heed to malicious slander – from the first, Soviet Man behaved like a romantic idealist, he wanted nothing more or less than goodwill and justice for the whole world and the whole of Mankind at once. But for a start it was necessary to destroy this and that, to rebuild anew. . . .

Since then much has indeed been built, albeit not very successfully, and anyway it is insignificant compared with that which was destroyed. And it was destroyed completely, professionally – so that not even the grass would grow. To this day Soviet Man has preserved the exalted perspective of the reformer, the builder of a new society. We know each other by this facial expression, as well. All that is missing is a minor detail – a mandate, signed by Feliks Dzerzhinskii, granting full powers merrily to reconstruct the whole world 'using any means, with the right to shoot on the spot'.

Translated by Martin Morgan

9 Can You Win at Chess with a Marked Deck of Cards?
Nora Buhks

Anatolii Gladilin is a writer of the Aksenov generation. His name is associated in our minds with the liberating air of the 1960s, the rise of Soviet Modernist prose with its special sensitivity to language, and new stylistics, marked by a distortion of officialese and youth jargon. This literary generation preached 'pure capitalism', 'ideal materialism', and a faith in the defeudalising power of the principle of material interest.

The writers of the 1960s, pro-Western and pro-American, defined their perceptions of the West in emigration, and realised them in different ways in their works about the West. Gladilin published his story *Frantsuzskaia Sovetskaia Sotsialisticheskaia Respublika* in 1985, that is, after living nine years in Paris. This would presuppose a close acquaintance with the country. The story belongs to the genre of political detective story. The plot concerns the establishment of Soviet Power in France, planned and partly carried out by the KGB. The form and plot of the text define the level of permissable juxtapositions and dictate the devices of decoding. Therefore I have decided not to compare Gladilin's portrayal of the Western world with those of other émigré writers, a superficially attractive approach, given the theme of this book. It seems more appropriate to me to examine the image of the West presented in the story in the context of the genre and the technical literary devices associated therewith.

The plot chosen by Gladilin is categorised in the Western literary canon as 'The Russians Are Coming', and possesses a rich bibliography in virtually all European languages. If we exclude from consideration articles and monographs of true or pseudo-scientific worth, which on the whole limit themselves to the past or present and steer clear of prophecy, although not always, then we are left with pocket paperbacks designed for reading on train-journeys. The characteristic device of this genre is discovery, which allows the reader to discover who is who and what is to come without much mental effort. Many writers in this genre seek a minimum of three endings. One is – 'to have no victors'. Statistics shows that this type of novel is much less popular with the public.

To put it plainly, Gladilin's plot is not new. Moreover, the author does not hide this:

> The French imbibe tales of KGB intrigues with their mother's milk, they put them on the level of television entertainment . . . Thousands of articles have been written in the West about the Soviet, Bulgarian and East German secret services. Has this changed anything? No, the Westerner in the street does not want to believe all of this, it suits him better and makes his life simpler.

This comment is vital for defining the author's position. This accusation of social egoism directed at Western readers is based on the ideological tendency of the genre (no doubt to the surprise of its readers and writers), that is, the genre has an openly propagandistic function. It is difficult not to recall Lenin's celebrated article 'Party Organisation and Party Literature', which proposed exactly such a function for literature. The whole of the French arts is subjected to analogous restrictions in Gladilin's story. For example: 'Not one genuinely anti-Soviet film was shown in France. Right-wing writers prefered to investigate the "mysteries of love"' (p. 53). The basic principles of criticism allow one to define opposing principles, perceived as correct and faithful to the historical setting. These propose the ideological subjugation of art of an anti-Soviet character. This absolutely ignores the fact that ideological commitment excludes creative freedom. One need hardly refer to examples in Soviet literature.

Gladilin's story does not neglect the Western man in the street, either. He takes one of the Leader's sayings as an epigraph:

> The so-called cultured levels of West European and American society are not capable of understanding the contemporary scheme of things, nor the real relations of power; these layers ought to be considered deaf and dumb and treated as such. No matter what they are told, the deaf and dumb believe it. Telling the truth is a petty bourgeois prejudice. A lie, on the other hand, can often be justified by the aim. (p. 7)

Although all of the preceding narrative confirms the great Lenin's prophecy, the West as portrayed by Gladilin is really deaf politically, although by passing into the orbit of the quotation, the work itself becomes clearly ambivalent.

One way or another, by choosing such an obviously hackneyed plot Gladilin seems to have committed an act fraught with risk and dictated by the author's view of the socio-political tasks of literature. The author's word is confirmed by Soviet experience, which acts as a kind of guarantee. One can suggest that this element raises the story above the rank of others of similar subject-matter, and gives it the function of an alarm-signal. Such a reading allows the introduction of real historical facts and personages into the narrative along with fictional ones. This applies for example to references to the French Socialists' seven-year rule, and Mitterrand's expulsion of forty-seven Soviet diplomats from France in 1983. Giscard d'Estaing can be seen in the portrayal of the French President (p. 101), as can Andropov be seen in the General Secretary (p. 21).

On the other hand Gladilin's position as a writer from 'over there', an outsider in French literary circles, gives his critique a note of parody. One can say that Gladilin's story parodies not only the West, but the Soviet world and, ultimately, the detective-story genre itself.

The first signs of parody can be seen in the portrayal of the protagonists. We see in the story a selection of clichéd characterisations, always balanced by similar treatment of the antagonists. I shall cite a number of examples. Gladilin portrays the French in their traditional role as womanisers ('they always "cherchent la femme"', p. 42), who take political decisions in their mistresses' beds, and economic decisions in strip-joints. The Soviets, on the other hand, regard the sexual act as no more than another Party task. Thus the KGB officer Zotov has an affair with Lida, a Soviet agent, only after Colonel Beloborodov's insistent request that he 'abuse his official position' for the sake of the conspiracy (p. 85). It may be noted, incidentally, that in the works of Gladilin there is a tendency to give Chekists names associated with the colour white. In the story *Repetitsiia v piatnitsu* (Paris, 1978) we come across Beloruchkin and Belokonev, while in *FSSR* we meet Beloborodov. All three are colonels. The symbolism of these names contrasts with the professional duties of their bearers. But let us return to sex. If, as Gladilin suggests, the French do not display the 'mysteries of love' (p. 94) (the right-wing authors did not strive in vain), then the Soviet agent perceives the striptease as a psychological attack. Zotov feels like a Soviet Adam in 'Eve's' striptease cabaret:

I worried that the girl on stage might remove her underwear; if only she would leave that gleaming triangle there between her legs. My KGB colleagues were right. I really am a theorist, quite unprepared for serious practical challenges. But, to my relief, the gleaming triangle stayed in place. (p. 45)

To move our sights a little higher, Gladilin asserts that the freedom-loving French are slaves to their stomachs. They pay more attention to gastronomic than to state laws. For example, when the first two Soviet divisions, one tank and one motorised, enter France, they find that near Verdun 'their path is blocked by twenty moustachioed veterans weighed down with field decorations from the Second World War' (p. 105). Clearly they had leapt to the defence of the Motherland. But then:

the tank drivers laid out their travelling mess table. With an expansive gesture the officer invited the veterans to sample Russian vodka and black caviare. The veterans rounded off the meal with a glass of vodka, but found it a little warm. The officer apologised – alas, tanks are not equipped with fridges. The veterans were given some souvenirs of the occasion and went their separate ways home. (p. 106)

An extract from the account of tankdriver Malofeev:

I popped into a shop, took it all in and thought a bit. I saw nothing I recognised, no vodka, no sherry, just shelves of some Guerlain or other. But it looked like strong stuff. So I just took three half-litre bottles and split them fairly with my comrades. (p. 136)

It is not difficult to see that the French in the story seem to be made of papier-mâché, but even this stereotype is rather overdone. The clear inference is that the French ought to abandon their gastronomic and sensual pleasures in favour of anti-Communism. Thus are the stereotypes subjected to ideological stereotyping in turn.

Gladilin's art of parody not only mixes the images of the protagonists, but also their conflict, in favour of caricature. In this case not only the descriptive tone of the parodied text is held up to ridicule, but the subject as well. Ridicule lowers the level of veracity, and the story degenerates into parodic literature.

The attempt to parody the genre itself leads to analogous results. It amounts to Gladilin's rejection of the basic organisational principle of the detective-story plot – unpredictability. This rejection is made twice, moreover: first of all in the title, which anticipates the conclusion, and again in its very composition. The narrative consists of the confession of the retired KGB man Zotov who, having told the reader how it will all end, goes on to tell him how it all took place. It is the obvious compositional realisation of the slogan 'The Victory of Communism is Inescapable' that turns a terrible warning to the Western reader into a joke.

One can perhaps add to the sum of Gladilin's parodic devices the violation of the traditional proportions between the various compositional elements of the political detective genre. Thus, the seizure of power, usually the shortest part of the denouement, becomes the longest in Gladilin's hands, making the action, as in slow-motion filming, not so much alarming as comic. I shall cite one more example of thematic parody. The machinations of the KGB are played out like a game of chess, and the actual operation is called the 'French Gambit', and its master-mind 'the chessplayer'. This reference to chess seems to give the actions of the KGB an intellectual character, and victory confirms their intellectual supremacy. But the chess analogy is not maintained, the type of game changes constantly. Thus the beginning of the game is played out like chess, but 'loser takes all' seems to prevail later. For example the KGB frame their own Colonel Fedorov and betray him to the French secret service, bomb the Soviet Embassy, and kill the General Secretary of the French Communist Party, all to deflect French attention from their main aim.

As the narrative unfolds, the game of chess turns into a game of cards: ' "So we had three trump cards", thought Zotov' (p. 52); ' "I guessed that the Ambassador was playing trumps, as I myself had given him the card . . . We beat them with a marked pack" ' (p. 61). Even billiards make an appearance later: 'The time had come to pot the black' (p. 55). Such confusion involuntarily changes the KGB from a serious intellectual opponent into a cardsharp, and the reader evaluates its real potential for danger accordingly. It is noteworthy that the Soviets' mate at the end of the story heavily colours the narrative style, through its punning ambiguity, being in practice the only proof of this semi-political, semi-fictional prognosis.

It is quite difficult to see that this hackneyed parody of a plot can be given an ideological reading. As before, the 'deaf' hear nothing, because the siren does not sound. But let us turn to another hypothesis. As our starting-point let us take the ultimate aim of the story –

the social response that Gladilin hopes to provoke with his critique of hallowed Western freedoms. The well-worn plot ensures automatic perception of its aim in the mind of the reader who, having read the book, discovers the truth about his own attitudes. By giving the functions of narrator to a Chekist, Gladilin adds weight to the action, and the very fact that the summary of the situation is made by the KGB turns it already into a plan. It is worth noting that the first factor to contribute to the KGB's victory was the activity of the intelligentsia: '"The whole of the left-wing intelligentsia worked in our favour", mused the hero, "moreover they worked for free. They set public opinion in the country . . . The young were educated by the left-wing professoriate . . . Oh yes, there were right-wing papers and journals, but who read them?"' (It is interesting to speculate as to who financed the right-wing press if nobody read it.) 'It was clear at the elections that half the country voted for the right, but the electors vanished down their burrows once the count was over, and the left-wing Thunderers once more took centre stage' (p. 53).

The division into left and right has long since lost its political and agitational meaning in the modern world, but it is retained in this story to define the ideological opponents, immediately raising doubts about its convincingness. While criticising the French inclination towards idle politicking, the narrator, contrary to all of his conclusions, dismisses the electoral results with a characteristic gesture and gambles all on one card. And yet 'The French are legalistic', as he notes later, 'they are brought up in a spirit of parliamentary democracy and constitutionality' (p. 137), and so for them elections are not a theatrical gesture but an expression of their civil rights and opinions. However, it is this very faith in Democracy, according to the narrator, that saps their initiative in history's decisive moment.

French social 'ills' are marked out in bold print in the text: 'Military service was ridiculed. The police were treated with open hostility. "Capitalist" and "factory-owner" became terms of abuse. The word "patriot" was a synonym for "arsehole"' (p. 54). These accusations can be summed up in one major criticism. In this story the West is blamed, as it were, for not being a mirror-image of the Soviet world. For only such an openly anti-Communist state can oppose the powers of Communism. Alas, in both cases freedom must be excluded *a priori*. The accusations of blindness and weakness levelled at French society are, once taken out of the context of the story, in fact indicators of the freedom of that society: freedom of expression, contempt for political extremism, the right to criticise the state security apparatus and even the right to describe the 'mysteries of love' and not the 'mysteries of politics' when it suits you. Western Man, so harshly criticised in the book for his hearing defect, in actual life displays the basic habits of a freeman, preferring seriously to consider his opinion rather than to erect fortifications in a panic. Ignoring something leads to demystification, reduction to a secondary level. It is not a coincidence that the narrator is revolted by the sight of the 'festive Parisian crowd' (p. 44), whose indifference pushes him to the periphery.

And so, is this work of Gladilin's a warning to the free West, calling on it to renounce its freedoms? This would be, in the author's own words, 'a strange anomaly' (p. 37), and thus not likely to be the case. This makes *FSSR* yet another piece of light reading for the masses, albeit with a familiar but amusing plot. Moreover, there is nothing wrong with this, especially if one agrees that literature has more aims than the purely ideological.

Translated by Martin Morgan

NOTE

1. Anatolii Gladilin, *Frantsuzskaia Sovetskaia Sotsialisticheskaia Respublika* (New York, 1985) p. 63. All subsequent page references in the text are to this edition.

10 Raisa Orlova-Kopeleva in Germany / Nikolai Nikolaevich Poppe in America

Hans Rothe

'Emigration is and always has been a misery', wrote the late Raisa Orlova in a book published in Germany where she had lived with her husband Lev Kopelev as expatriates from 1980 to 1989.[1] Her remark seems to be so self-evident that it may sound trivial, like many other things that have been said about misery in general and the misery of emigration in particular. In this case, it seems however that it might be useful to investigate the trivial.

In order to avoid misconceptions it has to be said right from the outset: Orlova did not want to emigrate. Her husband, Kopelev, was allowed to leave, and so she went with him. She did not want to go to Germany whose language she did not speak. She rather wanted to go to America whose literature she had studied and taught and in whose language she was fluent. Apparently this was yet an effect of the pre-Stalin 1920s, the years of light-headed self-uprooting, and of a credulous reaching beyond Europe. Orlova did not know Europe. It was for her husband's sake that she stayed in Germany. She learned to speak German fluently, an admirable accomplishment for her years. Actually she had to learn what Europe meant. A longing for Russia consumed her day and night.

She does not say it anywhere, but it is wholly clear that for her emigration could only have political reasons. But even for our century this is a quite one-sided restriction. Gauguin no less than Turgenev was certainly not a political émigré. Dostoevskii had to leave Russia because he was in debt; Goncharov wrote his last two novels in the West, because he did not manage to write a single line in St Petersburg; Mosche Altbauer left Poland in 1935 because he wanted to live in the land of his forefathers in Palestine; Ibsen lived for decades in Paris simply because it pleased him; and so on. It is advisable to leave this one-sided political point of view from the beginning.

It is, doubtless, a particular feature of our century and especially of Russia that émigrés meet with earlier émigrés, that for instance the Third Wave meets the Second. They suffer their mutual judgements. I will begin with the judgement of a man of the Second Wave of emigration,[2] a Russian poet and scholar who now lectures on Russian literature in California, concerning the Third Wave. As a Soviet prisoner of war he remained in Germany, married, and went to America. I do not know anyone with a finer aesthetic sense or a more profound expert on Russian poetry of the twentieth century. Without any attention from the public he had to make his way under the conditions of the post-war period. His attitude to the Third Wave is reserved. He once said, 'They think that they can eat oranges without picking them. We had to pick them, got some money and found our job in this country!' Found our job – that means: we found our life in this country. Certainly, this is the judgement of a man who has found a job and who does not need to pick oranges any more.

Every émigré will tend to view his life – positively or negatively – in an absolute way. At any rate he will act at the moment of irreversible decision, in the instant of crossing the border as if he definitely had reached 'the other side' and wished to stay there. Aleksandr Gertsen (Herzen), who was a major hero of Orlova, has given a literary shape to this attitude and it is this shape Orlova imitates in all her writings. Its essential feature is not the unalterable decision; it only seems so. The essential feature is rather the incessant occupation with one's self. And this almost inevitably leads to writing. Orlova says, 'On 12 November 1980 we arrived in Germany. On the 13th I wrote my first letter home. Since then I have been writing continuously' (*Türen*, 15). It was exactly the same with Gertsen. The most frequent word in her writings is 'I'. With her it is as with her greater model: whatever she describes, she herself is her favourite hero.

One will tend to regard this attitude – like the judgement about the misery of emigration – as immediately felt, caused by some pressing, immediately experienced distress. That there is such distress is undisputed; everyone who is forced to live outside his native country knows that. But still the literary historian had better remind himself of the fact that both – the judgement on misery and the monomaniac occupation with one's self – are elements of a literary tradition that stems from the literature of sentimentalism. Beginning with Karamzin, this tradition, which originated in England and was subsequently influenced by Rousseau and Goethe, affected Russian literature and has never quite left it since. Again it was Gertsen who was particularly pervaded by it and thus gave a literary shape to the fate of emigration through it.

Émigré literature is for a good part the literature of sentimentalism, and, as such, confessional writing. Orlova's books are replete with confessions. Being still at home she already lived partly in a strange world, had turned to an inward emigration. It is from this inward emigration that her inclination towards further confessions stems.

For the date 1961–84 she writes, 'the first eight post-war years were the most shameful of my life' (*Vergangenheit*, 429) and for the years 1975–7 we find, 'all of us who have deceived' (ibid., 354). The year 1953, we learn, meant 'awakening' (ibid., 429). This, too, is a literary topos originating in the literature of sentimentalism. In the 1860s it was so pervasively used by Russian critics that Goncharov – against all his own experience and against all the facts – was led to describe his novels as the shaping of sleep and awakening. For this reason Gertsen chose for his most important journal the title and epigraph of Schiller's 'Glocke': he wanted to rouse his readers from sleep, and this is just what Orlova constantly wants to do. Following this tradition Anton Chekhov chose a similar picture in his 'Kryzhovnik' (1898): a man with a hammer should continuously knock at people's door, at their hearts, to shake them out of their lazy drowsiness. This picture is also again and again quoted by Orlova.[3]

Whoever writes confessional prose of this kind takes a considerable risk. Very quickly there will be someone willing to find out whether the author has really examined themself critically, and as a rule they will find secret corners where no light has been shed. So it happened particularly to Rousseau, whose *Confessions* were ridiculed by Heine and Dostoevskii. It is certainly one of the major achievements of Russian 19th-century literature, mainly of Dostoevskii and to a lesser degree also of Tolstoi and Chekhov, that they unmasked the '*homme de la vérité*' Rousseau called himself and that Gertsen wished to pass for, as a poseur, a myth, almost *the* myth of the new era and that the topoi, motifs, and in fact the literary forms of all literature of sentimentalism are wholly insufficient for a critical, always repeated self-examination which, after all, is the major task of all literature, not only that of émigrés. There are mainly two examples of émigrés of our time who have accomplished this task and they were able to do so not by open confession but in the first place by using the alienating instruments of irony and cynicism directed against themselves. They are Thomas Mann's *Doktor Faustus* and Solzhenitsyn with his books.

And what about Orlova?

To begin with I will give only one example. In one of her confessions we find the statement, 'I got to know only after coming here that fourteen million Germans were driven from their homeland after the War and that two million of them lost their lives' (*Türen*, 32). (In reality about three million died.)[4] So this is a judgement about her own fate: expatriation and emigration. A man of my country and of our generation is experienced in dealing with the question of 'who knew what and when', and so I may ask in turn whether the author thought that Germans were allowed to continue to live in the territories allocated to Poland and the Soviet Union in 1948? Didn't she know about the end of the Germans in Bohemia and the Volga Republic?

I have chosen this example deliberately; not only to show the incompleteness of Orlova's confessions but in the first place to show the crucial point of all confessional literature in a certain provocative manner, namely guilt. May someone who is not free of guilt himself question an author of apparently such good intent so severely? May, in fact, any outsider interfere in such a way? Orlova reacts very irritably to 'severe judgements from outsiders' (*Türen* 157), and – being already in emigration – thereby draws on a topos that is known in Russia and especially in Soviet Russia since Pushkin's 'Klevetnikam Rossii' (1832).

But are there any outsiders?

Orlova describes an instance. An American historian, lecturing with undisputed expertise on the Russian Civil War, none the less aroused her indignation. 'Like a biologist', she tells us, he had 'observed with cool-headed attention' Russian affairs 'under the microscope.' His undertone had meant: 'The Russians have deserved all this'. So this is a quite complex instance, since the outsider is an expert betraying himself by an 'undertone' as an ignoramus. He represents the type of the narrow specialist all of us know. Orlova's judgement is that 'it is not easy to listen to severe judgements passed by outsiders who, although they rely on Russian research, give their categorical dictum condescendingly' (ibid., 157). No, it is not easy indeed, as everyone knows who has been entangled in guilt and must listen to just *and* unjust passing 'severe judgements'. But it is inevitable. Who cannot suffer it has not yet experienced what guilt in this world means.

It amounts to a denunciation of the outsider to mention experts who 'are concerned with Russia as their subject, from eight to five, so to speak'. In contrast to this she 'is attracted to those foreigners who . . . [are called] "Russians *honoris causae*"' (ibid., 161). Here too, it is sentimental enthusiasm.

Let us consider this enthusiasm for a moment. In strange contrast to it is the excommunication of the outsider. For Orlova says she has been raised with the ideal of the general fraternisation of all men. Through many remarks one learns that this ideal has always remained valid for her. To her 'human hearts and epochs are transparent', generations and epochs are able 'to understand each other'. 'Accessible are . . . dreams, delusions, and vain hopes . . . Possible it is for the grandchildren to share the joys, sorrows, and passions of the grandparents'. Hence she says, 'As long as my hand is able to hold a pen I will try to tell how we lived' (*Vergangenheit*, 430–1); and then the 'all-important question' . . .: 'Can people belonging to different worlds know and understand each other? . . . my hope is: building bridges is possible' (*Türen*, 217). Orlova is a passionate builder of bridges. Again Gertsen is her model who, we are told, is without precedent in the 'relations between Russia and Western Europe' (*Glocke*, 9).

But if this ideal exists then there are no outsiders.

This might be the appropriate place to remember the judgement of Theodor Fontane, the finest German author of the late nineteenth century, rarely read in Germany and almost unknown outside it. Born in 1819, he was nearly a contemporary of Gertsen. He says;

I have experienced many things that gave me deep inward pleasure . . . Among these glories . . . belongs the ever more apparent failure of the spurious wisdom of the past century. The misery that Lessing caused with his tale of the three rings . . . is tremendous. The "Embrace ye millions" [in Schiller's 'Lied an die Freude'] is rubbish. Sovereign tasks that cannot be solved are merely confusing mankind.[5]

This is a declaration of war against German Idealism's uncritical sentimentalism and by the same token a declaration of war against the sentimental idealism within Russian literature that we find in Orlova.

I will give yet another example of this peculiar contradiction between sentimental enthusiasm on the one hand and the rejection of

'severe judgements' on the other, between outsiders and certain
experts on the one hand and honorary Russians on the other.

Very often Orlova passes judgements on other émigrés. In
America she visited the widow of Leon Feuchtwanger in California.
Orlova believes that the German emigration after 1933 is not comparable to her own fate; according to her, the German émigrés had
an easier life because they had to leave their country for only twelve
years. 'In contrast, Feuchtwanger's life as an émigré took place under
the most agreeable circumstances imaginable' (*Türen*, 110). In the
article on emigration by A. Kantorowicz she might easily have
looked up how agreeable Feuchtwanger's flight from France had
been.[6] Did Orlova ever have to flee in such a way? And when she
came to the West, she reports herself that there 'were opened so
many doors that our life span will hardly be sufficient to enter
everywhere' (*Türen*, 103). It was in fact the case that not one married
émigré couple could be named, who again and again were so wel-
comed with open arms by the public as well as by innumerable official
and private persons, so supported and pampered, as the Kopelevs;
and they achieved immense public influence.

Misconceptions, to the point of real injustice, are numerous. I will
mention only one. The irritation with prosperity, and with affluence
and waste here is a topos in all reports by émigrés. This is irritating to
many of us too. However, a certain limit is transgressed when charity
organisations, such as the churches and the Red Cross, collecting
regularly for the poor throughout the world, are denoted as integral
parts of the so-called '*Wegwerfgesellschaft*' (throw-away society)
(ibid., 70–1). Of course, Orlova delivers this with the utmost sincer-
ity. I mention it to show the contrast with the following more clearly.

This contrast depends on the doctrine of the 'other Russia' which is
developed in much the same way as the idea of an 'other Germany' of
half a century ago. It is here that Orlova's tone becomes a few grades
more determined. She says that 'Russian culture exists' (ibid., 189).
And she says: 'We come from a country with a high culture' (ibid.,
49). Astonishingly, it is not the great literature of the nineteenth
century that is cited to substantiate the claim, but rather Soviet
literature over and over again, the knowledge of which is, we learn,
absolutely necessary for 'the West' (ibid., 159, 163). The culture of
the 'circles' is praised in all detail (ibid., 50 et ff). Beginning with
Pushkin, practically everything is supposed to have taken its start
from them (ibid., 52). These circles, we are told, are the institution of
inward emigration to which one turns when life is unbearable. This is

certainly credible, but never and nowhere has it been otherwise.[7] As a further example of how we are in need of high Soviet Russian culture, 'Bakhtin's discovery' is mentioned (what is meant is his carnival hypothesis), constituting a light for the West (*Türen*, 41 et ff). Nina Berberova (of the first emigration) is quoted: 'We are not in exile, we are messengers'. As regards herself, she says, 'I am in exile. With the inner commitment to give evidence' (ibid., 214–15). So there it is again, the sentimental literature of confession.

Demands on oneself and others can easily change to sentimentalism. The apogee is reached with a more detailed description of Russians *honoris causae*. Among the experts, we learn, there are not only those who concern themselves with their subject 'from eight to five, so to speak', but also others who love Russia. The English historian Geoffrey Hosking may hold different opinions, but 'he loves Russia'.

The Slavist from Geneva, Georges Nivat, is thorough and capable, 'and he loves Russia'. We find similar remarks concerning the Proffers of the Ardis publishing house (ibid., 152–4).

By now we would like to ask: why is this so? We are told constantly that many translations of Soviet literature exist, 'but much more has yet to be done' (ibid., 155). Why? I wish to avoid misapprehensions: it belongs to a proper civilisation that one is able to learn what is written and read in neighbouring countries to the East, that one may examine for oneself what the people of a country that had reached the heights of Pushkin and Dostoevskii are interested in today. There must be an opportunity for that. But it does exist already. Everyone, literally every one of us, is able to inform themselves. This is, even today, different in Russia. You have to translate and teach. But whether someone reads and learns is the decision of the individual. There cannot be any *must*. I want to go even further: the fact that I read the terrible things written by Valentin Rasputin or Varlam Shalamov, does not automatically heighten my culture; that I perhaps refuse to read them may be a sign of cultural diligence, in the sense in which Goethe refused to read Kleist. I admit that anyone who does not read Dostoevskii will never learn something indispensable about themselves. But are there still many Dostoevskiis to discover?

And why should we love Russia? Why should someone love anybody who is very different if he does not want to? Does that not amount to claiming a special role for émigrés, for Soviet literature, for Russia and all her circles? We know the misery of émigrés. We know the grievous torment of having to live far away from one's home. But is this the point? If we do not have compassion as we should, it is our problem. Their problem is longing, perhaps; but when they write about us, their problem is neither grief nor their special role, but rather their judgement.

If someone awakens, as Orlova puts it, one would like to know whether he really is awakening or whether he would like to continue dreaming with one eye open. If someone is settling accounts, one would like to know whether the account is correct. The most important question is the one about the Soviet Union's Socialist system of life. Again and again we read that Stalinism is criminal and that one feels communal guilt for it. It has been known for a long time that a mass murderer as leader of state is really nothing but a murderer. Should not the examination be extended to the system as such, including its birth, the Revolution and its midwife, Vladimir Il'ich Lenin?

As before, I want to avoid misapprehensions: of course it is possible to be a Socialist or even a Communist, just as it is possible to be a Christian even after the religious warfare of the sixteenth and seventeenth centuries. But it is certainly not possible without asking whether the injustice of Stalinism is not perhaps rooted in the Revolution and its ideology.

There is something else in this context that has not been mentioned. Orlova was a writer, and literature was her subject. But she writes about it with the pretension of a universal validity for Soviet literature, for high Russian culture. She tells us about 'the unusual witness of art' (ibid., 117). In this point she is absolutely right. If we consider the fact that German literature after the end of dictatorship in 1945 sank to a deplorable mediocrity and is still sinking deeper and deeper year by year, and if we further consider the fact that Russian literature has been led to monstrous degeneration through Stalin and Zhdanov, it is a miracle that it made its way again to such a high level by its own strength. But art alone does not make culture, and art alone is not sufficient as a witness of history. The question should be permitted: where are – in Russia and among the émigrés – the judges and lawyers who are unwilling to suffer the continous breach of law which Etkind has described so vividly? And where are the physicians who cannot allow medical institutions to be used as houses of correction for those who are dissenters, reported among other things by Grigorenko? Or those who protest against the catastrophic medical care for the population? Many more such questions could be asked.

My impression is that this sort of émigré literature is prefigured in the literature of sentimentalism. The model is incapable of solving the questions all émigrés have to suffer. The main question is: am I also responsible for the state of affairs in my country which have led to my being forced to leave it? With no less a person than Orlova's great model, Aleksandr Gertsen, it turned out that all his sentimental reports led to nothing but an ever more ramified and complex system of self-compassion and self-excuse. There is no-one who remained in this literary tradition with whom it has been otherwise. Many writers of the great period of Russian literature that was Gertsen's time perceived that his way of writing gives an incorrect view of East and West, and no less a person than Dostoevskii in his *Podrostok* has brought this home in all clarity. Among our contemporaries it is mainly Solzhenitsyn who takes up Dostoevskii's point of view anew.

Finally, I wish to draw attention to an émigré of the Second Wave. I do this in order to show that emigration and life outside one's home country can be differently understood and described. Nikolai Niko-laevich Poppe, born 1897, was and is the most distinguished scholar of Turkish and Mongolian languages and folklore. He is of Lettish-German origin, born in China, raised in Petersburg, attached to the Finns more than to any other people[8] and inclined to Russia and in particular to St Petersburg through his life, memoirs and his work.[9] In World War II he was captured by the German troops; as an interpreter to them he was able to prevent much misery and injustice, and on the withdrawal he went with them to Germany. From the beginning his intention had been to reach a free country, England or America. Finally he came to Seattle, where he still lives today. In 1982 he wrote his *Reminiscences* which appeared in 1983. His fate is that of a Soviet citizen and émigré. Unprecedented misery including death, persecution, poverty, grief, and separation is related by him in an extremely unbiased way, without any posture or mania for confessions. Whoever has had the luck to meet Poppe will never have the slightest doubt about his sincere, objective, humorous, and strong personality. (I learn that currently he is under attack in America. Only people who do not know him and his story could behave in such a way.)

In an essential point his *Reminiscences* are comparable to Orlova's *Türen* and several other émigré memoirs. Again and again Orlova says that her whole conception and way of life in the West depends upon comparison. I suppose this is not merely a habit but in the first place a way of making it possible to survive in a foreign country. To compare the right things is, of course, an art; but there is always danger that an émigré author will compare trivialities in a trivial manner. Poppe does not talk about it, although he, too, compares constantly, at times also trivialities, but his style is quite different. On several issues he arrives at the same critique of the West as Orlova: ignorance about the East, indifference, the economy of affluence. And sometimes he becomes much harsher, writing about the hypocrisy and treason of the West. He never becomes trivial or unjust. Above all, he never loses sight of the highest value: 'the greatest gift life can bestow on a human being, namely the gift of freedom' (*Reminiscences*, 254). We learn that as early as the 1920s he would have fled, if he could have taken his family with him. It was not misery and disaster that drove him out but injustice and lack of freedom. To him emigration was logical, although it was a misfortune; but it was still a small one in order to avoid a greater: 'I was offered an escape. Of course, Germany was not my final destination but only a stopover on my way to freedom. The way was long, with many delays and disappointments' (ibid., 285). These disappointments are rendered with great delicacy. He says that his professional success in America (against envy, ill will, and other adverse circumstances)

> has been the result of many favorable circumstances. Probably the most important of them is the American attitude of minding one's own business. I have been absolutely free to write as I please. No censors have imposed their ideas on me, no party members have 'edited' my works nor 'helped' me ideologically. I have never had any reason to protect my work from infringement, and there is no one in the US whom I would have to admonish '*noli turbare circulos meos*' (ibid., 260).

After having reported the latest unpleasant disappointments he had to experience in America, and after having related in a moving way the death of his beloved son and wife in dire but all the more touching words, he, being alone at the age of 85, writes;

> at present I am translating the Kalmuck epic cycle Jangar . . . my other research is of a linguistic nature . . . these lines are being written at the beginning of January 1982. It has been announced that this year's meeting of the Permanent International Altaistic Conference will be held at Uppsala in June. If nothing unexpected happens, I plan to attend it. Being in good health, I assume that

the 'unexpected' could be either lack of travel funds or some international political trouble. The latter has frustrated many of my plans, but I hope that I will be able to go to Sweden. (ibid., 293)

Could a report be more simple, unpretentious and clear, and thus more convincing? Is it possible to write more clearly about emigration and misery? And how could we be viewed and judged more discreetly under Eastern eyes?

NOTES

1. Raissa Orlowa-Kopelew, *Die Türen öffen sich langsam* (Munich, 1984) (paperback edition, Goldman Verlag, 98387) (hereafter *Türen*), p. 100. Other books by Raisa Orlova referred to in this paper are: Raisa Orlowa-Kopelew, *Eine Vergangenheit, die nicht vergeht. Rückblicke aus fünf Jahrzehnte* (Munich, 1983) (paperback edition, Goldman Verlag, 98570) (hereafter *Vergangenheit*); Raissa Orlowa-Kopelew, *Briefe aus Köln über Bücher aus Moskau* (Cologne, 1987) (hereafter *Briefe*); *Als die Glocke verstummte. Alexander Herzens letztes Lebensjahr* (Berlin, 1988) (hereafter *Glocke*). All English quotations are translated from the German versions of these works.
2. Vladimir Markov, who kindly allowed me to mention his name.
3. For example, *Türen*, p. 72.
4. Heinz Nawratil, *Die deutschen Nachkriegsverluste unter Vertrieben, Gefangenen und Verschleppten* (Munich, 1986), p. 32.
5. Theodor Fontane, *Briefe an seine Familie* (Berlin, 1905), pp. 73–4: 'Ich habe vieles erlebt, das mir eine tief-innerliche Freude gemacht hat . . . Zu diesen Herrlichkeiten, an denen meine Seele lutscht wie an einem Bonbon, gehört auch der immer mehr zutage tretende Bankerott des Afterweisheit des vorigen [i.e. 18.] Jahrhunderts. Das Unheil, das Lessing mit seiner Geschichte von den drei Ringen angerichtet hat, um nur *einen* Punkt herauszugreifen, ist kolossal. Das "seid umschlungen Millionen" ist ein Unsinn. Hoheitsaufgaben, die doch nicht gelöst werden können, verwirren die Menschheit nur.'
6. Alfred Kantorowicz, *Exil in Frankreich. Merkwürdigkeiten und Denkwürdigkeiten* (Hamburg, 1983), pp. 109–35.
7. Orlova does not shrink from associating herself with Goethe by describing his setting out for Italy in 1786 as a flight 'from order to the unordered' and by giving her 'awakening' of 1953 as an analogy: *Türen*, p. 87.
8. Nicholas Poppe, *Reminiscences*, edited by Henry G. Schwarz (Seattle, 1983), pp. 21, 258.
9. However, see *Reminiscences*, p. 8.

11 My i Zapad – Aleksandr Zinov'ev's View of the West

Michael Kirkwood

The title of this chapter is perhaps slightly misleading in the sense that many of the statements about the West which can be found in Zinov'ev's books must be attributed to his characters, not to himself. On the other hand, his own views are stated in a variety of essays, interviews and lectures which have appeared since he came to the West in 1978. It is also the case that the year 1978 is a watershed in that there are, not surprisingly, discernible shifts in emphasis, indeed changes of view, in what he has written since then which contrast with those which are detectable in his works written before he came to the West. We have to deal, therefore, with a range of perspectives on the one hand and a 'before and after' situation on the other.

What follows is a discussion of the picture of the West as it emerges from an examination of as much of Zinov'ev's *oeuvre* as I have been able to assemble. This includes all the books he has written since *Ziiaiushchie vysoty* up to the present, with the exception of two he has published in a language I do not read, namely, Italian. The West in Zinov'ev's view is predominantly the guardian of civilisation, is incapable of understanding the Soviet Union, is oblivious to Soviet preparations for war and is drifting in the direction of Ibansk, while as yet being the source of everything material that the Soviet Union requires. On the other hand, it also represents a threat to the inner workings of Soviet society. In other words, we observe a dialectical tension between the West as being in some sense the prey of the Soviet Union, the latter representing Communism in its classical state, and at the same time the West as a destabilising factor in relation to the smooth running of Ibanskian, that is, Soviet society.

Before embarking on our analysis, however, we must address the issue of the pace of change in the Soviet Union and Eastern Europe at the present time (January 1990). Current events taking place in the Soviet Union suggest that the main destabilising factor is ethnic tension rather than Western influence, and that if anything Ibansk is drifting in the direction of the West rather than vice-versa. In this context much of what Zinov'ev has written and said appears to have been overtaken by events. The massacre at Tiananmen Square, however, reminds us of the more familiar face of Communism and it is not yet impossible to envisage a resort to force by conservative elements in the Soviet Union were Gorbachev to be removed. Zinov'ev has always maintained that a Communist society is incapable of reforming itself, and it remains to be seen whether he is wrong to think so. It is possible, indeed perhaps even probable, that it is precisely the mechanisms of Communist society which Zinov'ev has described which are the fundamental impediments to the success of Gorbachev's programme of reforms.

In the remainder of this chapter we shall address two issues. Firstly we shall consider the range of views which can be assembled from a review of the treatments of the major topics, including those which can be directly attributed to Zinov'ev himself. Secondly we shall consider the extent to which Zinov'ev's view of the West has been influenced by his experience of living in it for the last eleven years.

THE WEST AS THE GUARDIAN OF CIVILISATION

One of Zinov'ev's most important ideas is that when sufficiently large numbers of people live in the same environment for a sufficient length of time certain 'social laws' come into operation which regulate people's behaviour. They are most succinctly encapsulated in the formula 'dog eat dog', or in Russian '*Chelovek cheloveku – volk*'. Civilisation, argues Zinov'ev, is the history of attempts by societies to restrict these social laws by the invention of such phenomena as morality, law, art, religion, the press, *glasnost'* and public opinion. These views are first expressed by Shizofrenik in *Ziiaiushchie vysoty*. In *V preddverii raiia* an episode in the Boy's diary includes a discussion of the relative merits of individualism and collectivism. It is agreed that in the West society is often indifferent to the fate of the individual, but it is argued by the Boy's chance acquaintance that that indifference is the extreme, negative consequence of the very positive phenomenon of the legal and moral defences which protect the individual in the West from the abuse of power and from society.[1]

The earliest statement of Zinov'ev's own views on this question which I have found is in an interview for Radio Liberty conducted in August 1979 and reproduced in *Bez illiuzii*. In response to the question of what impressions he has gathered from his first year in the West he says, *inter alia*:

> I have no illusions about the West and I see its defects. But it is the best of all that has been in the history of mankind and is the best that there is on the planet at this moment. The West is capable of developing civilisation and has the strength to stand up for itself.[2]

There is quite a lot of discussion of this topic in *Zheltyi dom*. In the first volume we find two of JRF's egos nicknamed Zapadnik and Vostochnik debating the likely outcome of the ongoing struggle between the two systems. Vostochnik regards the West and the East as two different civilisations. The difference between them is similar to the difference between climbing and falling. Climbing requires supportive measures and effort, falling does not. It is easier to fall than to climb. For Vostochnik the problem for the future will be how to live on the planet when the Eastern civilisation triumphs. For Zapadnik the problem of the struggle between East and West is a social one and is a struggle which is conducted both in the West and in the East simultaneously. For Zapadnik the problem of the future will be how to retain a few crumbs of Western civilisation under the new order.

The view that the West is the guardian of civilisation is also expressed in the course of at least one of the night-time conversations that take place in the rest-home outside Moscow which is the setting for the final part of *Zheltyi dom*:

> 'What is civilisation based upon? On the principle that you earn your daily bread by the sweat of your brow. What, however, does Communism promise? In disguised form nothing more than a paradise of idleness?'

Later on the same speaker avers:

> 'For the moment we are living off the creative energy of the West. And because of that we still muddle through one way or another. But what will happen when the West is destroyed and takes the same road as us?'[3]

The answer he receives is the following: 'You might get endless decline or centuries of stagnation'.[4] In another conversation, just before leaving the rest-home, JRF and his New Friend touch on the subject again:

New Friend: 'Our [i.e. Soviet] society was formed along many parameters with the result that the process is irreversible.'
JRF: 'But was there any one unifying factor in that process?'
'Of course, the socialisation of the means of production.'
'Do you think the same thing will happen in the West?'
'It will if there's socialisation of the means of production.'[5]

It is well known, of course, that Zinov'ev published in 1981 a series of articles, interviews and lectures which he gave during the years 1979–80 under the general title *My i Zapad*. The idea that the West is the guardian of civilisation under onslaught from negative forces epitomising Communism is central. Here is a passage from his article 'Vostok i Zapad' which echoes the metaphor of climbing and falling which we have already encountered:

Civilisation in general means effort, clambering upwards, going against the current. The East in its current historical phase supports the opposite tendency, namely taking the line of least resistance, going with the current, slithering downwards. What can the West promise those millions of people living in deprivation or who would like more than they've got? Only the instruments of civilisation: physical and intellectual labour, moreover over generations. What, however, does the East promise? Destroy the source of your misfortune – Western civilisation, and you will gain everything![6]

The eponymous hero of *Gomo sovetikus* agrees: 'The current situation in the West is the pinnacle of what mankind can achieve in every respect, it is an exception to the monotony of history.'[7]

THE INABILITY OF THE WEST TO COMPREHEND SOVIET SOCIETY

This is the charge that Zinov'ev never tires of levelling at the West. It has been a source of intense irritation to Sovietologists especially, most of whom, as a result, no longer pay any attention to him.
Probably Zinov'ev's most scathing device is the depiction of the

well-disposed Western intellectual who conscientiously meets with Soviet intellectuals 'off the record' and discusses various aspects of Soviet life, appears to sympathise with them, then goes back to the West and writes a book about the Soviet Union which presents it in a much too positive light in the opinion of said Soviet intellectuals. This device is first employed in *Ziiaiushchie vysoty* in the string of texts devoted to 'Journalist'. It is again used in *Zheltyi dom*. For Zinov'ev the basic difficulty in understanding social systems is not in the sphere of data collection or statistical processing but in discovering procedures for comprehending the normal everyday experience of social beings. As Teacher puts it in *Ziiaiushchie vysoty*: 'The main difficulty in the understanding of social phenomena . . . [is] . . . finding a means of understanding the commonplace.'[8] This attitude, of course, puts Zinov'ev on a different plane from economists, historians, political scientists and sociologists, who have to work within the particular paradigm of their chosen discipline. Zinov'ev uses intelligence, experience and his own observation of human nature, eschewing the more conventional methods of the social sciences. Nevertheless, working on some plane in between the literary, ethical, socio-political, and philosophical, he contrives to say things about the Soviet system that ring true.

The device of the visiting Western intellectual meeting disaffected Soviet intellectuals informally has its counterpart in the visiting Western academic, politician, or other VIP who appears on Soviet television and politely endorses the regime by not criticising it directly. Having watched an aristocratic English banker in an interview on Soviet television praise various aspects of Ibanskian life, Physicist has this to say:

> What is he, a cretin? Or is it some kind of calculated behaviour? I don't know. Surely it doesn't escape these degenerates that when they act like that they collaborate with our masters and voluntarily assist in digging their own future graves?![9]

Zinov'ev in his postscriptum to *Zapiski nochnogo storozha* states that his characters touch on the problem of relations with the West and says that they do not understand westerners. He goes on to say:

> And I too, I have to confess, fail to understand them. Not long ago I heard a married couple from the West who had spent a year in the Soviet Union being interviewed on the radio. They praised our way

of life to the skies. Do they really not realise that they have no experience of what our life is actually like? They had no problems with accommodation, foodstuffs, getting their kids into higher education, making a career, getting their work published or exhibited. They didn't have to chase around the shops, stand in queues, fight their way on and off public transport, sit through meetings, vote for inane proposals, struggle to find official or unofficial means of getting away for a holiday. Do they really not realise that their remarks make them collaborators with our authorities and propaganda and help the very people who are going to bury them? And yet there are many such foreigners. And what characterises their behaviour more? Stupidity? Irresponsibility? A secret predilection for our way of life?[10]

It does not occur to Zinov'ev that the most likely explanation is common courtesy and a desire not to cause unnecessary offense. On the other hand, the charge he levels at foreigners is to my mind a serious one. None of us Westerners has experienced Soviet life as it really is for any length of time. How can we understand it, as Soviet citizens understand it?

There is another aspect of Western incomprehension of the Soviet Union which Zinov'ev finds more sinister. As far as I can ascertain it is first adumbrated in *V preddverii raia*. Foreign visitors from the West have been listening with ill-concealed boredom to stories of camp atrocities, repressions, and so on, then throw up their hands in disbelief at tales of queues for lavatory-paper, tales which they consider to be anti-Soviet propaganda (*VPR*, 374). This is a point which Zinov'ev will develop in later works in great detail, in *Zheltyi dom, My i Zapad, Gomo sovetikus, Moi dom – moia chuzhbina, Ni svobody in ravenstva in bratstva, Der Staatsfreier, Para Bellum, Ruka Kremlia, Gorbachevizm.*

It is his belief that the KGB discovered during the 1970s that people in the West quickly came to terms with Stalin's atrocities, indeed became bored with repeated descriptions of them. Moreover, they were willing to be deceived by the Soviet Union in ways which suited them. That is to say, many were won over by various Soviet peace initiatives. People in the West wanted to believe that people were much the same everywhere. The result was that the old Khrushchev-era emphasis on how Russians were different and the Soviet system superior has given way to emphasis being laid by Moscow on how similar we all are, how our differences are much less important than our similarities, how we are all inhabitants of the same global village, and so on. In this light Gorbachev is merely carrying out a policy whose guidelines were set by Andropov.

Although the majority of the examples of Western incomprehension of the Soviet Union describe naïve foreigners in general, or Sovietologists, quite a few make fun of the Western left-wing intellectual. There are two reasons. Firstly, left-wing intellectuals continue to believe in Marxist 'fairy-tales' about equality and justice in a post-capitalist world. Secondly, they regard the Soviet experience as irrelevant to Marxist theory. Here is one response to the idea that Eurocommunism (remember Eurocommunism?) might be conceivable as Communism with a human face:

> In the first place, I was born in the Soviet Union and have lived there for more than fifty years. And what Communism is I have learned not out of books written a hundred years ago, not from looking out of the windows of the 'Intourist' restaurant, not from conversations with leaders of the CPSU, not from newspapers, not from the shop-windows of 'Berezka' shops, but as it really is. In the second place I am not a politician but a scientist. And as a scientist I can assure you that building 'Communism with a human face' is about as possible as flying to the moon on a samovar sold for hard currency to tourists from the 'Berezka' shop I already mentioned.[11]

Matrenadura is typically scathing in her remarks about Western Marxists:

> 'My nephew says that they believe in Marxism over there. Not like over here. Over here they laugh at it . . . but there they believe in it! Treat it with respect. There's culture for you! They even respect Marxism!'
> 'Why "even"?'
> 'Why do they want to respect it? If Marxism lays its hands on power over there, confiscates everyone's property, dumps folk in jail, they'll end up with just as big a mess as we've got. What's the point of respecting it? But they do.'[12]

WESTERN OBLIVION TO SOVIET PREPARATIONS FOR
WAR

This is a theme which gives Zinov'ev almost as much cause for
concern as the West's inability to comprehend the true nature of
Soviet society. The earliest reference to this topic which I have
noticed arises in the course of one of the many conversations in
Matrenadura's barn. JRF, SRF, Ivan Vasil'evich, Lob, Don Kikhot
and company are discussing various aspects of the West and finally
touch on military matters. There seems to be general agreement on
the essentials. It will take about two days to seize Europe, and most
of that will be spent destroying Yugoslavia and West Germany. The
rest of Europe will, as his phrase has it, fill their trousers and
surrender. I remember some years ago seeing a newspaper report
about a Danish defence policy proposal by some youth organisation
or other, possibly students, which was encapsulated in a placard in
Russian saying 'We Surrender'. Perhaps Zinov'ev saw something
similar. At any rate, he has a very low opinion of Western youth as
regards their willingness to defend Western capitalism, the guardian,
one recalls, of civilisation itself. Switzerland might offer some resistance, but it is too small to count. Apart from Western disinclination
to fight, however, there are other factors which favour a Soviet
victory. There are thousands of Soviet agents in the West, and a fifth
column of tens of thousands. There will be millions of volunteers.
Everything will depend on the Americans.[13]

   In a later conversation the same participants discuss another aspect
of what Zinov'ev regards as Soviet preparations for war, namely the
current wave of emigration to the West. This topic is no doubt a
source of some of Zinov'ev's unpopularity in émigré circles. JRF's
view is that the current emigration is a Soviet penetration of the West
which merely takes the form of emigration, moreover the form of
escape from an inhuman regime to the free world. Soviet people
remain Soviet wherever they are, and in the West they are the
advance guard of the Soviet army. Another question which is discussed in the same conversation concerns the will to win. Again the
balance of advantage is seen to lie with the Soviets, since the West
has too much to lose, does not live from hand to mouth as is the case
in the Soviet Union. The Soviet Union, on the other hand, is used to
crisis, living on the brink, sacrifice.[14] JFR's views are summarised by
himself in a night-time conversation with his New Friend:

'And yet the West's days are numbered', said JRF. 'Why? Because destroying the West is our *idée fixe* . . . Secondly, because all the dungheaps in the West are acting in our interests. The youth of today. Backward nations. Not to mention Communists. Even businessmen who have dealings with us are digging their own grave one way or another. Thirdly because we undeviatingly adhere to the principle of penetrating the countries of the West by any means at our disposal. Our "fifth column" is already fifty times stronger than Hitler's ever was.'[15]

It is perhaps significant that I have found no particular treatment of this topic before Volume II of *Zheltyi dom*. I may, of course, have missed the occasional reference in *Ziiaiushchie vysoty*, *Svetloe budushchee*, and so on, but certainly in those earlier works there is no obvious and repeated treatment. Volume II of *Zheltyi dom* was written after Zinov'ev came to the West. One recalls that the years from 1979 till the mid-1980s formed the period during which NATO's so-called 'twin-track' policy was in operation and bitterly, if unsuccessfully, opposed by a variety of European peace movements. West Germany, in particular, was the scene of many large demonstrations which opposed the installation of Cruise and Pershing missiles. Zinov'ev, sitting in Munich, was probably appalled by what he saw and heard. Certainly the theme of Soviet preparations for war is one of the most important threads running through *Gomo sovetikus*. Indeed, one could argue that the whole book is devoted to that theme. The same could be said for *Der Staatsfreier*, *Para Bellum*, and his play *Ruka Kremlia*.

The theme also occurs in *Moi dom – moia chuzhbina*. One of the central characters is a Soviet apparatchik who is ordered to go to the West as an émigré with his wife Niushka. Niushka's view of the West is actually worth a paper all to itself. She is the quintessential provincial Russian wife and is a kind of urban equivalent of Matrenadura in *Zheltyi dom*. Her views on the West are down-to-earth, pragmatic, innocent of any hint of cultural, historical or philosophical influence. She has not been in the West for long before she becomes worried about Western defence policy towards the Soviet Union, a worry she shares with her husband:

And Niushka starts off again.
'Van', we've got a problem:

How are we going to live here in peace?
We need to arm the West.
Otherwise, our lot will come
And take all we've got.
Did you and I suffer in vain?
Did you and I go hungry for nothing?
Was it for nothing that we . . .?'
And on she goes like that.
I try to take refuge in my study.
But there's no salvation there either.[16]

We have concentrated so far on the West in a geo-political sense. Zinov'ev, however, treats the West in an important sociological sense and we shall try now to restore the balance somewhat by considering the extent to which Zinov'ev believes the West is of psychological importance as a factor in everyday Soviet life.

THE WEST AS A FACTOR IN SOVIET EVERYDAY LIFE

Zinov'ev treats this topic on several levels. For instance, there is a material sense in which the West is an everyday factor in Soviet life, namely the fashion for Western goods of virtually any description. There is also a prestige factor to be considered. Travel to the West and invitations to Western conferences convey prestige on those fortunate enough to have the opportunity. They are by definition trusted by the authorities, are likely to benefit in career terms, they have access to foreign goods, and so on. Then there is the propaganda factor. The various '*vrazhdebnye golosa*' such as Voice of America, Deutsche Welle, Radio Liberty, the BBC, provide a steady stream of information about the West in addition to a steady stream of information about the East which renders the notion of an Iron Curtain not only obsolete but ridiculous. This Western influence, which is widespread and growing, engenders a corresponding ideological response. Thus Soviet propaganda is to a large extent influenced by the need to counteract the effects of pervasive Western influence, especially among the young.

Zinov'ev devotes a separate chapter in his book *Die Macht des Unglaubens* to the West in Soviet ideology. In the ideological context, of course, it is the 'corrupting influence' of the West which is of most importance. Zinov'ev argues that this 'corrupting influence' is no invention of the propaganda machine or of the KGB. It really exists and has to be taken very seriously. As he says himself:

> The West has become a permanent factor in Soviet everyday life. For the next two or three generations at least the notion of an Iron Curtain is unthinkable. The West has entered the consciousness of the Soviet individual via many channels, among which undisguised ideological anti-Soviet propaganda and propaganda in favour of the Western way of life are the least important.[17] (*DMdU*, 192)

Later on he adds that the West had dealt a formidable psychological blow to the internal workings of Soviet society, its '*vnutrenniaia zhizn*', or *Innenleben*, and has fuelled corruption at all levels, especially among the young in the middle and upper strata.[18]

We now come to the last question to be treated in this paper, namely the extent to which Zinov'ev's views have changed since he came to the West in 1978. In the last eleven years he has been interviewed many times, has delivered countless lectures, written countless articles. Three volumes containing some of these have appeared over the years: *Bez illiuzii* in 1989, *My i Zapad* in 1981, *Ni svobody ni ravenstva ni bratstva* in 1983. I have already quoted Zinov'ev's own words in defence of the West as the guardian of civilisation. Yet his approval is by no means uncritical. This is clear from a passage in a lecture he gave sometime between 1980 and 1981 and which is reprinted in *Ni svobody ni ravenstva ni bratstva*. He is addressing the topic of 'Western ideology', a concept with which I was previously unfamiliar. Among other things, he says the following:

> People in the West don't want to admit that they too are being systematically made fools of by ideology . . . I'll quote a few examples of Western ideological ideas . . . . The advocacy of sexual promiscuity, pornography and depravity in the guise of various forms of culture, of the body, of sex, of human relations, of science, medicine. The advocacy of marital infidelity, violence, gansterism, parasitism . . . . The criteria for distinguishing between the significant and the trivial, between honesty and hypocrisy, between the praiseworthy and the contemptible are being systematically undermined . . . Moral values are seen as being old-fashioned and are accordingly treated with derision . . . Western ideology, like its Soviet counterpart, is destroying the instru-

ments of civilisation fashioned over centuries as a means of restraining the unruly forces of man's social environment.[19]

If Western moral fibre is not as strong as Zinov'ev would like it to be, it is at its weakest, in his view, in the face of what he regards as the permanent Soviet threat. The two themes of Western inability to comprehend the true nature of Soviet society and Western oblivion to Soviet preparations for war are present in several of the works which Zinov'ev wrote while still in the Soviet Union. It is notable, however, that since he came to the West these two themes have acquired central importance. *Gomo sovetikus* is his first full-length treatment of the psychology of 'Gomosos', apparently a contraction for Gomo Sovetikus, but of course a pun which suggests parasitism. The two central messages of that work are that: (a) *Homo sovieticus* remains *homo sovieticus*, even in the West; (b) the emigration known as the 'Third Wave' is the advance guard of the Soviet invading forces. As one of the characters says:

Earlier we came here as heralds of the weakness of the Soviet system; and we strengthened hopes of its imminent collapse from internal causes. Now we come as heralds of the strength of the Soviet system, as the vanguard of an attacking army.[20]

These same two themes receive full-length treatment likewise in recent works such as *Para Bellum, Der Staatsfreier, Ruka Kremlia*. There can be little doubt that Zinov'ev's earlier, pre-1978 perception of what he regards as Western weakness in the face of the Soviet threat has become a central preoccupation since he has come to the West. In this respect the advent of Gorbachev and *perestroika* has done nothing to change his mind.

We are now in a position to essay a conclusion. As I have tried to show, Zinov'ev's view of the West is multi-faceted. For him the West is as much a sociological and psychological phenomenon as it is a geopolitical one. That is to say, he views the West not just as something external to the Soviet Union and threatened by it, but also as a phenomenon which has infiltrated the Soviet environment and which threatens it in turn. On the other hand, there is an ongoing, never-ending struggle between the forces which characterise the 'West' and 'East', a struggle which takes place in both territories. For Zinov'ev what differentiates the 'West' from the 'East' is a long list of slight differences, differences which, however, *in toto* add up to fundamentally different societies. In his writings Zinov'ev seems to give the balance of advantage to those forces which characterise Soviet society. On the other hand, he has not given up hope entirely and would probably still stand by what he wrote at the end of *Kommunizm kak real'nost'*:

> Mankind's switch to Communism is not just a new play in a theatre performed by the same old actors. The actors themselves have changed and they will have to act out the old plays in a new style and to invent new ones of their own.
> Well now, Homo sapiens, what happens from now on is up to you alone! Show what you are good for, O Highest Form of Life![21]

NOTES

1. *V preddverii raia* (Lausanne, 1979), p. 91.
2. *Bez illiuzii* (Lausanne, 1979), p. 118.
3. *Zheltyi dom* (Lausanne, 1980), II, p. 351.
4. Ibid.
5. Ibid.
6. *My i Zapad* (Lausanne, 1981), p. 20.
7. *Gomo sovetikus*, (Lausanne, 1982), p. 94; *Homo Sovieticus* (London, 1985), p. 96.
8. *Ziiaiushchie vysoty* (Lausanne, 1976), p. 337; *The Yawning Heights* (London, 1979), p. 494.
9. *Zapiski nochnogo storozha* (Lausanne, 1979), p. 33.
10. *Zapiski nochnogo storozha*, pp. 111–12.
11. *V preddverii raiia*, p. 434.
12. *Zheltyi dom*, pp. 119–20.
13. *Zheltyi dom*, pp. 103–4.
14. *Zheltyi dom*, pp. 131–2.
15. *Zheltyi dom*, p. 316.
16. *Moi dom – moia chuzhbina* (Lausanne, 1982), pp. 115–16.
17. *Die Macht des Unglaubens* (Munich, 1986), p. 192.
18. See *Die Macht des Unglaubens*, pp. 196–7.
19. *Ni svobody ni ravenstva ni bratstva* (Lausanne, 1983), p. 50.
20. *Gomo sovetikus*, p. 120; *Homo Sovieticus*, p. 124.
21. *Kommunizm kak real'nost'* (Lausanne, 1981), p. 230; *The Reality of Communism* (London, 1984), p. 259.

12 Émigré Experience of the West as Related to Soviet Journals

Julian Graffy

I

To observers of the rapidly accelerating opening-up of the Soviet press in the years since 1986, the position of émigrés has offered a particularly sensitive gauge. The publication of the writings of émigrés is an *a priori* expression of a degree of liberalisation – one that was not achieved at all in the period of the Khrushchev 'thaw', with which recent developments were initially compared. The (almost exclusively posthumous) publication of works by émigrés of the First Wave began in 1986.[1] But the return to print of living émigrés, ready and able to express their scepticism about the process that was underway, was an undertaking fraught with potential embarrassment, and Soviet editors approached it with understandable caution. In March 1987 one of the first signs of a new readiness to tolerate diverse views was the publication in *Moskovskie novosti* of the notorious 'Letter of the Ten' (émigrés) which had just appeared in prominent Western newspapers such as *The Times* and *The New York Times*, and which expressed grave reservations about Western euphoria over developments in the USSR.[2] In December of that year publication of a selection of poems by Iosif Brodskii closely followed his receipt of the Nobel Prize for Literature.

The years since 1988 have seen a stream of publications of prose and poetry by living émigrés mainly in liberal journals and newspapers. Interest in émigré views and experience has also been reflected in literary criticism; in articles about life in emigration; in reports on a series of recent meetings between émigré and Soviet intellectuals in Louisiana (Denmark), Barcelona and elsewhere; and in newspaper columns and articles commissioned from writers such as Voinovich, Siniavskii and Kopelev. A large number of émigré artists and writers have made much-publicised return visits to the USSR. Some, such as Sasha Sokolov and the ex-director of the Taganka

115

theatre in Moscow, Iurii Liubimov, have returned for longer periods. The veteran (First Wave) writer Irina Odoevtseva returned permanently in April 1987.[3]

In the context of this heightened interest, the (written or oral) interview with émigrés has become a prominent genre in the Soviet press.[4] Since these interviews offer émigrés the opportunity for direct expression of their views, they have been considered worthy of detailed examination.

Predominantly émigrés have been interviewed in the 'liberal' organs that have been directly implicated in the opening up of the Soviet press: in newspapers such as *Argumenty i fakty*, *Knizhnoe obozrenie*, *Nedelia*, *Moskovskie novosti* and *Sobesednik*: in the weekly magazines *Ogonek* and *Novoe vremia*; in such 'thick monthlies' as *Iunost'*, *Druzhba narodov*, *Teatr* and *Iskusstvo kino*. These organs are also involved in the publication of the writings of émigrés and studies of them. Interviews have been systematised by the introduction of rubrics such as 'O tekh, kto okazalsia na chuzhbine' ('On those who found themselves in alien lands') in *Nedelia* and 'Russkie v Parizhe' ('Russians in Paris') in *Knizhnoe obozrenie*. In its February and March 1989 issues, the journal *Inostrannaia literatura* set thirteen émigré writers and critics (some of whom had not yet had their literary works published in Soviet journals) four questions on the literary emigration and their views on Soviet literature.[5] At this stage there still seemed to be a tendency to divide émigrés into 'good' (i.e. sympathetic towards the course of events in the USSR) and 'bad'. In this context it is not surprising that the first interview with Vladimir Maksimov did not appear till the end of 1989.[6] At the time of writing, it is only the most prominent émigré of all, Aleksandr Solzhenitsyn, who has given no interviews to the Soviet press, though his lengthy manifesto for Russia has just appeared in two Soviet newspapers.[7]

A wide range of attitudes is apparent in these interviews, both to experience of the West and to Soviet developments. In part this is dependent on the circumstances of leaving the USSR. The majority of these people were pressured into leaving, but others left through marriage or to go to Israel. Most left feeling certain that they would never return to Russia, but some have been able to make regular visits. Age at the time of leaving is also a factor. As might be expected, writers feel particularly strongly about having to live and work outside the sphere of the Russian language. It is also of relevance whether the interview took place in the West or in the emotionally heightened circumstances of a brief return to the USSR. What can be stated unequivocally is that the overwhelming majority of interviewees emerge with dignity from these encounters. While they almost invariably express love and concern for the country of their birth, they also go to great pains to inform Soviet readers of the repression and humiliation that in many cases preceded their departure.[8] Nor are they reticent about the outrageous treatment some of them have received in the most recent period. (A particular cause of irritation has been the delay in returning their Soviet citizenship.)[9]

By contrast, interviewers, particularly in the early examples of this genre, do not hesitate to ask leading questions about the pain caused by separation from the native land. The word *rodina* (motherland) makes increasingly predictable appearances in questions, often in association with the words *u nas*. (Confusion over the words *my* [we] and *vy* [you] is recurrent – do émigrés still qualify as part of *my*, or are they now *vy*?) If the interview takes place abroad, the interviewer often seeks to present himself as an innocent: Feliks Medvedev cannot trace Brodskii in New York and cannot get hold of a car (Brodskii a); Anna Pugach is afraid to phone Aksenov since 'I knew from our fellow countrymen who had been abroad that Aksenov is not gracious to representatives of the press . . . ' (Aksenov b). An interpretative 'frame' can be used to place the interviews in the desired context. The *Inostrannaia literatura* questionnaire was published between an introduction by Chingiz Aitmatov and an afterword by D. Zatonskii which did not hesitate to criticise the 'mistaken' ideas of some interviewees and to single out others for approval. Thus Aksenov is berated for speaking of his 'self irony' and Zinov'ev for not finding any new work of Soviet literature to praise, while Korzhavin is commended for his warm words about village prose. The 'corrective frame' here can be compared with the use of emotional interpolations, for example by Egor Iakovlev, who informs readers of his interview with Iurii Liubimov (Liubimov a) that it took place 'in a night café of an alien [*chuzhogo*] theatre, in an alien town and in an alien country'. (The interview took place in Stuttgart.) Titles are used (sometimes misleadingly) to the same emotional end. Thus interviews appear under such striking headings as 'I cannot be separated from Russia' (Shemiakin a); 'Emigration is a terrible but instructive experience' (Siniavskii and Rozanova c); 'All my pain has remained here [in Russia]' (Voinovich d); 'Fellow countryman' (Nuriev a); 'In her native land' (Makarova a), 'I reside in the United States, but my soul is here in Moscow' (Fedorova a); 'I stood in the queue marked "for Soviet citizens"' (Orlova, a).

Gradually such tendentiousness has become less marked, though in a recent interview (Gavrilov b, p. 27) the pianist Andrei Gavrilov was driven to real anger by the unreconstructed 'true believer' stance of his interviewer, who was ready to accept that Gavrilov's foreign friends before his departure really were spying on him for Western intelligence agencies.

Perhaps inevitably, interviews have become increasingly absorbed with an assessment of the current woes of the Soviet Union, and émigrés are often tempted into the mechanical dissemination of the clichés about President Gorbachev's chances of survival, the state of the economy, the party-bureaucratic conservative opposition and other presently burning issues that the context almost demands of them. Nevertheless, they do also speak at length about their attitudes to the West. Much of what they say here, too, will strike Western readers as banal and predictable. They often seem insufficiently ready to acknowledge that their views have been coloured by their own position as outsiders in the West. They are sometimes too eager to display their knowledge to their Soviet readers. At other times they are only too ready to play to the prejudices of their interviewers or their audiences, indulging in a game of mutual flattery. It is only some, such as Vasilii Aksenov (b, p. 82), who are acutely aware of the dangers of generalisation and stereotyping. On the other hand they are frequently forthright and often amusing. And whatever their stance, the readiness to speak frankly and at length provides a great deal of information for assessing their own prejudices, and the effect their uprooting has had upon them. What is most absorbing and persuasive in these interviews is the recounting of personal experience of the West through 'eastern eyes'. There follows a survey of émigré statements.

II

The physical experience of emigration, often at very short notice, the emotional dislocation that followed it, and the beginnings of a new life are vividly recalled:

> Emigration is an agonising process. The first year is particularly agonising: at a particular moment everything starts to irritate you

madly, becomes hateful, you make generalisations . . . The worst bit of all is when you start making generalisations . . . (Aksenov b, p. 82).

I considered that my life was over and I was leaving to live out my days . . . when I found myself abroad I felt that life there was also unbearable . . . (Korzhavin b).

Emigration for me was a compromise, it was provoked by exhaustion . . . (Korzhavin e, p. 47).

The most terrible thing is when you turn out to be nobody – not out of work, not a beggar, but simply NOBODY (Limonov a).

It's very difficult to survive here . . . Emigration is terrible. It's loneliness, it's constant mutual recriminations . . . (Liubimov a).

For me emigration is not paradise, for me it's an enormous shock. And I lost rather than gained. Maybe I live well socially, but internally I live very badly (Maksimov a, p. 84).

I didn't know a single word of English . . . And I began to feel this internal alienation – not towards Russia, but towards the Russian language. For example there'd be the *New York Times* lying there and a Russian paper. To read the *New York Times* is work, but to get the same information from Russian papers is pure pleasure. So I didn't make any use of Russian literature, I just felt enmity when I heard Russian speech, I thought I was being dragged down. Because it was already all a stage that had been cut off (Neizvestnyi e, pp. 79–80).

The temptation to go to seed and become nobody when you are cut off from the Motherland is very great, because in the West there are far more problems. Nobody helps you, you don't know the language. Everything starts from scratch. It's as if you're being fed on semolina from a spoon. You suddenly start looking at a world in which you must answer for everything yourself. Through your own work. Through your own life. Through your own word. Through your own signature. It's a very complicated and difficult life. And it's amazingly wonderful (Panich a, p. 25).

. . . I got my first contract two years later, and that gave me the possibility of renting a studio. But making a career in the West is definitely very hard, complicated. To survive abroad you have to struggle. For that freedom which I dreamt about, real, authentic freedom, the freedom which I am now approaching, you have to battle long and hard for that (Shemiakin e, p. 9).

When I saw the shops which sell everything for artists, I got quite neurotic. An unbelievable quantity of different paper, the like of which I'd never dreamt of . . . I was struck dumb because I saw a mass of appliances for art, for graphics, the purpose and aim of which I just didn't understand. I saw the same abundance in other shops of course, unknown products, I can remember they were selling the skins of some animals, leopards, zebras. I thought: my God, how long shall I have to go on learning just so as to understand the what, where, how and why of this life, so as to feel not even a person with equal rights, but to learn how to walk along these streets, to go into these shops (ibid.).

Emigration is an experience which you have to go through. Either you'll perish or you'll leave something behind you, do something. There can be no talk of victory (Siniavskii in Siniavskii and Rozanova a).

Emigration is a very interesting experience, a very terrible experience, but it's also instructive (Rozanova in Siniavskii and Rozanova c).

Wherever you go, you can only adapt to a certain degree. You can go to the bank, ride in a wonderful car, eat in marvellous restaurants, acquire the appropriate lustre, externally turn into a foreigner, but only externally. You'll be accepted in that society, but you'll remain Russian (Sokolov c, p. 200).

I found it very difficult to get used to things. The first three years I hardly wrote a thing, I spent all that time adapting . . . The troubles a writer encounters abroad are specific. But they're not material difficulties. The difficulty is the sense of being cut off from your native reader. A difficult psychological atmosphere . . . Emigration is also a trial which it's difficult but possible to pass through. In that case emigration, like any other circumstances in a writer's life, can enrich rather than impoverish his creative work (Voinovich a, pp. 82, 83).

For three years after I was deprived of citizenship I couldn't write a thing. I was just thrown off the rails, I wasn't psychologically ready, I found it difficult to get used to things (Voinovich d).

In the evening we went out into the town . . . I looked at Paris . . . The image of the town which I had formed from childhood from books and films was quite unlike the reality. Maybe because I was seeing it through the eyes not of a tourist, but of a person who had come here to live. A person with no social status, no means of existence, no friends. At one moment it seemed to me that I had committed a crime with regard to the family whom I had brought here. That there was no future; I would not be able to enter into the life of this city. That night I looked out of the window of my pitiful room in the hotel at a mass of lighted windows, and I had the terrifying thought: not one of them contains anyone who has any suspicion of my existence. This thought both oppressed me and forced me to gather my forces . . .
[My paintings] were obsolete, because they were false in principle. I had extremely imprecise ideas about what modern art was in general, and what was happening in the West in particular. In Paris I understood that the paintings I had brought were dead. I was like a man with a diamond in his pocket, who found himself on a planet where they were lying around on the ground like ordinary stones . . . everything had to be begun from the beginning. I had considered myself to be an artist from childhood, but if in Paris I had come to the thought that I was a bankrupt, I would quite simply have had to die. I studied painting for eleven years, I had an excellent schooling, but it was only in Paris that I began my own path (Zaborov a).

Our family spent several years in a state of shock when we found ourselves in the West. My wife Ol'ga and I went through a profound spiritual crisis. It took us almost four years to get out of it. For us expulsion to the West was indeed a heavy punishment . . . the move from Russia to the West for us was not simply a move from one country to another . . . but a move from a qualitatively different system of existence, another dimension of existence (Zinov'ev b).

There was a minor scandal in the airport. As is the habit here, I was met with the words: 'We greet you in the realm of liberty.' I answered that I did not consider the West to be the realm of liberty, that I had been a free man in the Soviet Union. Soon after that articles appeared in the émigré press: 'Zinov'ev has revealed his face', 'Zinov'ev is a Soviet agent', 'Mr Zinov'ev, what is your rank in the KGB?'. There was even a rumour, a very funny one, that Zinov'ev had been sent to the GULag, and the one who had come here was a KGB colonel.

We found it very difficult adapting to life here. For the first four years we were almost in a state of shock . . .

One of my heroes in my book *Homo Sovieticus* expresses my moods like this: 'I hardly feel any suffering over the loss of my relatives and friends, my flat in Moscow . . . But the loss of the collective gives me no peace either day or night . . . Any one of our (my) collectives. Here in the West there are organisations which are very like Soviet collectives, but . . . they don't give the individual the sense of being protected, the spiritual warmth you get from Soviet ones . . . It sounds comic, but here they don't have the party organisation, that highest form of intracollective democracy. I want to sit at a party meeting. I want to go on a *subbotnik*. I'm even ready to go to do some work at a vegetable base, go to a collective farm for the harvest' (Zinov'ev c).

III

Most of these people have now lived in the West for several years and are able to supply Soviet readers with more detailed and analytical pictures of Western life. Gavrilov's interviewer asks him about the current Soviet fashion for seeing the West as paradise on earth:

It's all rubbish. A primitive and very Soviet view. Soviet people think that all you have to do is emigrate and then simply paradise begins. Maybe it's the effect of our propaganda, maybe it's the reverse effect. For almost all Soviet people life abroad is a phantasmagoria. They don't understand a damned thing. Almost all Russians are monstrously bad at adapting. In the first place they can't slough their Soviet skin, they continue to hang around together, to spend their time in their own circles, they speak Russian, they're bad at coming to terms with the [local] language. If they are famous people, they are capricious, just as they were here [in the USSR]. They demand special attention. Many of them experience the most cruel disappointment, an absolute certainty that they have been misunderstood. They don't find themselves and many go to ruin . . .

All Soviet people are of the firm conviction that [in the West] you can earn a certain sum after which you can do nothing. Even here in Moscow the musicians ask me: 'Well, how are you doing, have you earned enough yet? Can you sit around doing damn all already?' . . . This fairy tale concept of Western life is probably caused by our parasitical nature. There probably aren't any greater parasites in the entire world . . . Everyone's shouting for someone to give him something . . . Maybe it's because of their slavery or because their initiative has been cramped. But one way or another this is why when our people begin to live in the West they suffer cruelly. And naturally they end up badly . . .

The whole charm of Western life is that if you work well you earn well. The Soviet émigré is the most unfortunate because he's the most molly-coddled person in the world, for all the difficulties of life here . . . He finds working and keeping himself in order very difficult (Gavrilov b, p. 29).

Others give similar warnings about the need to work hard in the West:

In the West a child must start earning relatively early, without regard to his parents' background or capital. This is a matter of honour – getting on your feet independently (Koreneva a).

I have to say that in the West people live more intensively, intensely in the sense of the work rhythm. Everyone simply works more (Voinovich d).

Several make positive general assessments of Western life:

I was never an absolute Westerniser [*zapadnik*], but in some respects the West turned out to be better than I had expected . . . in the West people have managed to create a definite material level for themselves; there are many cultural achievements, which should be appreciated, and which we should know about (Korzhavin e, p. 47).

The Germans are a businesslike, hardworking, practical people. A bit cold. What you'd call a Nordic character. The TV's beginning a series of films of German life. In five minutes the hero takes out his pistol, this is followed by the first punch-up, and you know there are going to be several. If you consider that art reflects life, well you'll not find that kind of life anywhere [in Germany]. The only person I've seen with a pistol was a policeman. If someone chances to knock the door of his car against the door of another car, there are immediately a thousand apologies. The Germans are uncommonly polite and extremely keen on sport. When they get together it'll be the strongest European power. I think the frosts of 1941 had a major effect on them, because they're always hardening themselves: they go around in winter without coats, they go for runs wearing vests (Vladimov c).

This is a life which some émigrés have attempted to succeed in despite all their initial difficulties:

An artist's life in Russia is very organised: everything's thought through, chewed over, and all he has to do, without any effort, is to swallow it all. Dancers are under constant protection . . . Everyone is used to someone doing their thinking for them all the time: the pioneer organisation, the komsomol, the regional party committee, the town party committee. In the Soviet Union they did everything for me too, so in the West at the beginning it was very difficult. Here you have to think for yourself, you're your own enemy and friend. For example in the London Royal Opera House the dancers don't even get a pension, they have to think for themselves about what they're going to do when they're forty-five or fifty . . .

[Interviewer] Don't you think that in general in the West art is more a question of entertainment, more superficial? That here ['u nas'] it has greater social significance, that people feel stronger emotions when they watch a show or a film?

[N] . . . In general the western public is better informed, it knows more, but we shouldn't get upset and miserable about that, it's just that the West has an older culture (Nuriev a, pp. 20, 21).

[Interviewer] Could we say that you have become a western person, or have you remained ours [*nashim*]?

[P] I have become your western person. I am convinced that people of my generation, of my circle are Westernisers. After all we were reared on jazz, on cocktail halls. Vasilii Aksenov has written wonderfully about that in *The Burn* and Aleksandr Kabakov in his jazz tales (Panich a, p. 25).

Other remarks are more equivocal:

Is it easier to work abroad? In some ways it's easier. You don't have to spend your entire time hiding your manuscript, as I had to do in Moscow. You have a well-organised, peaceful, measured life, but certain irritants which force you to write disappear. There's too much freedom, do what you want. I consider that freedom has its own burden. To write you have to be boiling in the human cauldron and knock against its sides. And [here] I'll never have Tvardovskii alongside me saying: 'Look, that's kid's stuff, it's not serious' (Vladimov c).

I once met Viktor Nekrasov in Rome. He started trying to per-suade me that you can adapt, that he himself had adapted long ago. But a few days later he and I were wandering around Paris on the day our mutual friend Aleksandr Galich died. And Nekrasov said: 'In Moscow I always knew everything about every passer by, but this fellow, this Parisian, I don't understand him: who is he, where is he going, the devil only knows . . .' (Korzhavin c).

I've heard that Sasha Sokolov has been speaking harshly about the West on Moscow television and in the papers.
 I can't say anything bad about the West. They gave me refuge here, they gave me a magazine, they publish me. In Russia I was starving, here I'm satisfied, I could go on in that tone, but there is a grain of truth in what Sasha Sokolov says (Maksimov b, p. 8).

. . . for me life there [in Paris] is like stereo cinema: you seem to see everything, everything is close up, voluminous, tangible, but all the same you're outside it. As Brodskii said most aptly about himself, I have moved only in space (Maksimov c).

Other views of the West, sometimes from the same speakers, are unequivocally negative, with particular scorn reserved for Western reading habits, and maybe with an element of flattery towards their Soviet readers. Certainly some of the opinions expressed here are forthright:

. . . in Paris and New York . . . as Khodasevich once joked bitterly, all they read is dream books and calendars (Glezer b).

I was never a Westerniser or an anti-Westerniser. In that sense I
haven't changed. But certain Western diseases have become more
obvious to me. The Western liberal intelligentsia is proud of the
fact that it is tolerant. I don't like the word tolerance. I prefer
another formula, 'Respect for the truth'. I don't consider respect
for the opinion of others to be essential – after all it's only a
manifestation of politeness. The only thing that's essential is respect for the truth. And respect for the opinion of others, without
regard to what that opinion expresses, is in fact indifference to the
truth. In the West you can often hear: 'Bear in mind that it's not
done here to talk about literature outside of working hours.' But
after all literature is something that completely devours a person.
It's not a professional subject. It's life. For them [*dlia nikh*] a
conversation about literature is the same as if you've gone to visit
someone and they force you to chop firewood. They have an
expression there: 'Too emotional.' But after all, thinking is an
emotional process. In essence this is again an appeal to indifference. This is not at all a feature of American life. It's a feature of
the western liberal intelligentsia, especially its academic part.
(Korzhavin b).

[Interviewer] Do you still hate the western way of life as at the time
you wrote 'Edichka'?
[L] 'Hate' isn't the right word. I just understand clearly that
Western civilisation is created for the average man, a completely
uninteresting man. It is inimical to creative people (Limonov d).

Life is very harsh here. Everyone looks around himself for where
and how to work. Of course, some of them don't manage to find it.
In Moscow they ask you such questions, some of them think that
it's almost manna from heaven here. I answer them honestly: oh,
brothers, it's difficult here (Liubimov b, p. 43).

You won't improve the West with satire. Shaking the foundations
of that life is senseless. Not because life there is ideal, but because
it can't be reformed. Development has reached the heights which
are accessible to human beings, and the system that has been

worked out, for all its flaws, satisfies the majority (Voinovich c, p. 29).

[On Marlen Khutsiev's film *July Rain*] It was phenomenal. It was a strange film. All the time before I felt the lack of such *strangeness*. I think that's why I left for the West.
[Interviewer] And did you find it there?
[S] Unfortunately not. It's there in the same modest doses as it is here (Sokolov b).

I never dreamt about western freedoms. Even without them I said and wrote what I wanted and I never dissembled, I never accommodated. And I also never dreamt about western material prosperity. My requirements on that account were minimal. I was more than satisfied with what I had . . . When I ended up in the West I didn't fit in there either. As *Pravda* wrote, I didn't become a millionaire. But the reasons for that are the same ones that stopped me becoming part of the privileged stratum in Russia. I could have become rich if I'd betrayed my principles, and set off down the path of compromise. In the West too people don't behave any better than some of my compatriots – all they want is to snatch a fattier chunk of goodies. Of course, western society has its undoubted merits. But they are by no means accessible to all. And they have to be paid for. Nothing is given free here. You can have a wonderful life here if you have enough money. But to earn it you have to go down into the nether world of society, which for a person like me is scarcely different from its Soviet equivalent.

And in the creative sphere there are defects here too. The West has its ways of punishing refractoriness. And those who get to the top are by no means always the most talented. In short, absence makes the heart grow fonder. I doubt whether Russian people in the mass would agree to put up with the defects of the western way of life for the sake of its virtues (Zinov'ev b).

Western scholars of Russian literature do not find favour:

In general in the West, I don't know how it is in the field of their own literatures, but as for Russian literature, they are helpless, helpless to a degree that I had not expected. These are their categories for assessing someone: either you're a third Pasternak or

a fifth Tolstoi, or a fourth Dostoevskii, a second Solzhenitsyn . . .
I've never read a single serious word about myself. And not only
about myself, about many people (Maksimov b, p. 9).

IV

Reactions to life in the USA are predominantly enthusiastic:

America is another planet (Shemiakin d).

I now live in America, I really love this country, or more precisely
the town I live in, although Americans consider that New York
isn't America, but I like this state within a state, it's a sort of
station or cosmodrome of the twenty-first century, where there are
thousands of dialects, customs, cultures, it's a sort of New Baby-
lon, and where no one takes any notice of anyone. And they have
no such concepts as the House of Creativity or creative work trips
paid for by the state, which the [Soviet] Union of Artists has.
    . . . And when I first came to America, I was shocked by the
brightness of the sun, you know the light is really like in India, not
like in Europe, and these handsome, laughing people are walking
around, and you have the feeling of total lack of constraint, an
extraordinary self-confidence and friendliness. I had already spent
a number of years in Paris so it made me neurotic . . . I got
neurotic because when I was in Paris, I felt that I was living in the
art centre. For Europe Paris is . . . Paris! And suddenly I felt, no
way! This is where you have to live (Shemiakin e, p. 9).

You can't just sit things out here. Here you've jumped into the
water from an ocean liner and you have to wave your arms about
so as to swim . . .
    I came to America. I liked America, so I stayed . . .
    In Europe things were simpler for me, people knew me as an
artist there. Why did I stay in America? The thing is, there is such a
concept as space. It's important, Andrei Tarkovskii and I discussed
it. Space is a spiritual category. When I felt that space, from
Alaska to New York, I understood that I'd find it easier to work
here . . .
    European space is so saturated with art-solution that Europeans
don't want to build anything that rises higher than the level of the

psychology of their space. That's European intellectual chauvinism . . .

. . . A true artist always operates not on a mundane scale but on a poetic scale. Unfortunately, Europe operates on a day-to-day scale . . . Americans aren't embarrassed by the idea of the grandiose, nor are Russians. And besides, there exists in America something which could exist in Russia if things developed normally there, a synthesis, an integration of cultures, that's what interests me. American spiritual culture integrates different elements of negro culture, Mexican, Russian, European. This stew hasn't yet formed into a concrete style, but the presentiment of a style is there (Neizvestnyi b).

What was remarkable for me about moving here? The fact that behind every bush is the ocean, and that gigantic breath of the ocean saying 'So what?' The ocean which compromises all that subdivision into little flats and little cages . . .

I'm not speaking as a settler, but as a nomad. It just happened that when I was 32 I got the fate of a Mongol. I listen; but I listen as if from the saddle. I hear about the fate of the settlers and their sufferings (Brodskii c).

You don't understand . . . We, my circle, we were more American than, perhaps, the Americans themselves . . . When I spoke about the idea of individualism, that was what we were dreaming of. And for us the only place where it was embodied was the United States. And we wanted to know as much as possible, at least about art, and we wanted to be Americans in the sense that we wanted to be in some degree individuals (Brodskii d).

[Interviewer] Did you want to go to America before?
[D] Yes. I won't say that I was a great Americomane, but I knew more about America than about any other country. And that isn't a matter of chance. Brodskii likes to keep saying that in order to live in America you have to love something in that country. I was lucky, I knew quite a lot. I always loved jazz. Strange as it may seem, I loved the American cinema. I loved American sport and I knew something about it. I loved American fashion, I liked American style. Like all normal young people of my age I loved Hemingway. And I loved American prose in general – it was the only literature about which I could say that I knew it, at least super-

ficially. And besides that, I knew something very important for me – that in any other country, let's say in Europe, I would be a foreigner. The only country in the world where a person of incomprehensible origins, speaking an East European language, can feel at ease is America. New York is a branch of the globe, where there's no dominant national group and no sense of such a group. I was so fed up of being I don't know what – I've got brown hair, all my life I've had a beard and moustache, so I'm not a Russian, but I'm not Jewish and not an Armenian . . . So I knew that I would feel good there (Dovlatov c, p. 28).

My first impression of New York: I woke up early in the morning and went out on to Fifth Avenue, though I didn't yet know what that signified. I felt like a cockroach which had gone out for a walk among the cupboards. I wandered around for a bit and then I ran straight back into the hotel . . . It's a very cruel town, but in a certain sense I'm in love with it (Limonov a).

. . . I've already got used to this country . . . I worked for a year at the Kennan Institute in Washington, we liked the capital and we decided to stay and live here. I didn't like New York, but here I really do work well. I treat this country as home, not as my motherland [*Rodina*], you'll understand that, but as home. They gave me refuge here, not a feeling of peace but a feeling of home. I don't feel out of place here, because there are millions like me, various refugees from the entire world (Aksenov b, p. 82).

[Interviewer] You have said that life in America gave you a certain cosmopolitanism.
[A] That concerns above all the American way of life. When I was living in Moscow, what did a Chinaman mean to me? Some slant-eyed person whom you don't understand, and all you feel is alienation. But in America a Chinaman is an inalienable member of American society. It's quite impossible to imagine American society without a Chinese cook, without Chinese cooking. We always eat in Chinese restaurants. It's the most tasty and cheapest food. But the Chinaman is not only a cook, the Chinaman is a remarkable architect, the Chinaman is your student. My seminar invariably includes a Chinaman, a Korean, a Vietnamese, a Pole. Although I'm Orthodox, I like going to the Catholic cathedral where Poles, Czechs, Filipinos and Irish are all sitting together.

There's a moment when they all turn towards each others and shake hands. And it's great when you are united in that handshake. Suddenly a human molecule is formed. And I value it greatly (Aksenov f, p. 11).

Here, among Americans, I've learnt a certain kind of reserve . . .

I've also learnt how to smile, at least formally, stretching the corners of my mouth. And that's not at all a bad thing. America teaches you that. Soviet critics usually call it the country of formal smiles. But when my mother went to Paris and was told that the French only smile formally, she answered: 'I'd rather have a formal smile than undisguised rudeness' . . .

Here I've felt a stronger sense of belonging to humanity. I've felt myself to be a member of humanity . . . I no longer feel stereotypical things about blacks, I no longer think of them as some sort of victims of oppression; I have different attitudes, human attitudes to them. This sense of America as an ethnos has widened my ideas, widened my world . . .

The members of the American intelligentsia I feel closest to are international journalists . . . In the first place they're first-class professionals, highly qualified. And secondly they have a very wide horizon. They're such cosmopolitan Americans. Each of them has a touch of Hemingway (Aksenov h, pp. 88–90).

I haven't in fact become Americanised. I shall never become an American, although I have become a US citizen. But I certainly have become more cosmopolitan (Aksenov k, p. 15).

Other Russians living in the United States have had greater difficulty adapting:

I think that in their emotional structure my films are more appropriate for our viewers than for Americans. Americans don't like any ambiguity, half tones, mixing of genres. For them a comedy must be a comedy, a hero a hero, a bad man must be bad. You can't have something where a man is good and bad at the same time, for example, which is what European and Russian culture is based on.

So practically all my films flopped in America . . .

The difficulty is that Americans are used to headlong pictures, but ours are all slow and long. And anyway Americans are educated to be prejudiced against anything Russian. It's difficult to surmount that. They see us through a certain prism of stereotypes . . .

In America I forgot about our Russian leisuredliness. When you're shooting there you can hardly catch your breath before they're all, ready for the next episode (Mikhalkov-Konchalovskii a, p. 7).

The whole of American life is very rational, and so it contains no place for contemplation. And in this lies a certain drama which happens quite often in Western life . . . That's the gap between generations and the inner sense of being orphaned. In short, America is a nation of orphans . . . All this brings about a certain reserve, a dryness in relationships. It's not in the American nature to cry, they don't respect it, they hide it, they're ashamed of it. When they part they just slap each other on the shoulder, they don't kiss like us. It's not done. There's a curious thing about them. Your neighbour will never knock on your door to borrow even a match. He'll only do it if he knows you very well. Let alone the very idea of asking to borrow money. There is an extreme respect for privacy. Breaking this is punished by a fine. In Switzerland, for example if you play music after eleven o'clock in the evening your neighbours will immediately phone the police without even giving you warning . . .

We could never behave like that. We're not a nation of solitaries. Here [*u nas*] a stranger can easily knock on the door and ask for anything at all, right up to 'have you got any grub?' (Mikhalkov-Konchalovskii c, p. 17).

In America there's a cult of strength. You always have to be in the stirrup. You absolutely mustn't be tired . . . The noble boyish 'don't beat a chap when he's down' doesn't work. Beat him! So I try not to be down . . . (L'vov a).

[Interviewer] I've sometimes heard your voice on Radio Liberty and I noticed that you never say anything offensive about our country.
[L] Huh, Lenia! You listen to what I'm going to tell you. Recently I took part in a discussion on TV. I said something good about Gorbachev. So then this famous American gets up and says, 'He's

a KGB agent!' So I immediately replied, 'Well, if I'm an agent of the KGB, you're almost [*sic*, JG] an idiot'. Just imagine, publicly, straight on to the air waves! . . . (L'vov a).

I started studying English . . . I listened to tapes with themes like 'travel', 'at the shops', 'in the restaurant'. I became intrigued, which one of them would include art? If you were making tapes for Europeans then art would come under 'history'. But in America it comes under 'in the house'. There were phrases like: 'You have bought a wonderful sofa, and hung a pretty picture above it.' That is to say the American mass consciousness treats art as an object to prettify daily life. Naturally my art was at odds with this (Neizvestnyi c, p. 48).

The reservations of the writer Sasha Sokolov about American life are already notorious, and have been set out at length in the Soviet press:

. . . you'll rarely see a library in a private house which has more books in it than there are rooms in the house . . . If it's true that 'In Russia a poet is more than a poet', then in America he is clearly less. For the reading public, or, to put it better, the public that does a little reading, belles-lettres have sense and meaning only in a political context . . . To achieve the favour of the notorious average American, whose house has approximately five rooms, the writer has to be socio-politically close to him, courteous. So you have to learn to play intellectual giveaway. God forfend that you try anything avant-garde, experimental – or what do you call it? Make it simpler! (Sokolov a, p. 245).

It's a fantastic country where there's absolutely everything. This makes life seem unreal . . . Only for all their prosperity Americans have forgotten about things that are no less important, they've lost the taste for them . . .
You know all those critical outbursts by Soviet journalists about the West? About their spiritual poverty, about the power of the 'golden calf', all those unflattering clichés. We didn't believe them . . . But now we've seen it and we can say from our own experience that the Soviet journalists turned out to be right about many things.
. . . The only trouble is that the majority of Americans are not

interested in other countries and don't know what goes on there,
what's happening in art, culture, literature . . .

. . . For me the American town is in many ways a desert. What is
a town for us, as we are used to imagining it? It's the possibility of
interesting acquaintances, meetings, new people who know something important. But here no one is going to open his soul to
you . . . Here someone else's soul is not so much an area of
darkness as that same private property, and nobody will let you
'walk' across it. Once, after I'd been living in America for a few
months, I saw . . . a girl crying at an automobile station. She was
standing there crying. I suddenly remembered that the world
contains tears, grief, some real emotions and tragedies. It's usually
easy to forget about that here. You have to live God knows how
long and where to see a person suffering. People and their relationships seem unreal, not to say defective. And not because they've
decided to behave in this way . . . this behaviour is formed by long
tradition, by the national spirit . . .

. . . They don't like complex books in America . . .

. . . Americans are a very tolerant, very flexible people, it's
almost impossible to quarrel with them.

. . . The majority of the public here are not interested in anything which is not directly connected to their work, to their life this
minute . . .

. . . I don't think that America could be called a flourishing
country in that respect [culturally], The taste for reading is dis-
appearing completely . . . In American schools they don't teach
you to learn poetry by heart. It's considered inhumane to force a
child to do what he doesn't want . . . You walk respectfully
through the magnificent halls of the museums here, but in those
halls you are almost alone . . .

. . . Death in America is outside the law. It's not done, it's
almost indecent to allude to it. It's tactless. Maybe by speaking of
the death of someone close to you you will upset the person you're
talking to. Why bother people with your troubles? Sort them out
yourself. Americans don't like thinking about unpleasant things.

. . . They don't have grave-diggers here, they have a machine
like the one used for laying pipes. It takes the coffin off the lorry,
goes down into the grave with it on its automatic arms and lays it
down there. Then a bulldozer smoothes it all out. Of course there
are no nails: neither the first nor the last, they've all been banged in
long ago. And no tears, no sobs . . .

. . . There is a complete absence of hysteria in love dramas and family dramas here . . .

Conversation here is reduced, the majority of people use 300 to 400 words . . . For us the word 'book' is associated with the concept of serious literature, but when an American says 'book' he can mean a guide to how best to water his vegetable garden or how to put his money in the bank . . . Or 'party'. For us it's a lively, sometimes stormy discussion of something that makes the heart beat faster, but for an American it means getting together to stand around feeling bored while languidly swapping meaningless phrases. I don't think a Russian (*rossiianin*) could really feel at home here (Sokolov c, pp. 196–7, 199–202).

America is an amazing country in the speed with which it forgets things. Literally a few days after an event people don't remember the names. No, they'll remember an explosion on a spaceship for a long time, but they won't remember any cultural events and pass them on by word of mouth. That happens only in Russia . . .

I lived for six months in a writer's home. He said: live here and feed my dogs. That's quite usual when people go away for a long time. I was dumbstruck: he had no books in his house. He is a very rich man, he's made a vast fortune out of a series of books . . . No, they read bestsellers, they do. But he didn't even have any dictionaries, any encyclopaedias, they don't know that in order to write you have to read . . .

. . .They have no respect for language, they have no habit of conversation. All they do is work, not knowing why, aimlessly (Sokolov d, p. 66).

V

'They have no respect for language . . .'. For the people being interviewed here, on the other hand, language is crucial. Hardly any of them have tried writing in English, and the work of Nabokov and Brodskii in that language is seen as exceptional.

Yesterday I finished a new novel, *The Egg Yolk*, I wrote it in English, can you imagine that? It took me three years . . .
[Interviewer] Can we say that you've decided to become an anglophone writer, or was this just an experiment?

[A] No, no, I don't intend to go over to another language. I just tried to write a novel as part of the process of improving my English. It was a profoundly shady, brazen enterprise (Aksenov b, p. 83).

I love language. Literature for me is play, not in the mundane sense but in a lofty and serious sense – Play. You might say that literature is the art of handling words. But it's not language in general that I love, it's specifically the Russian language. Theoretically speaking I could write in English. But there are things in Russian that are completely absent from other languages, and without which I wouldn't find it interesting. It's like depriving music of the semi-tones. There's no inflection in English, no cases, inversion is problematical. And on the other hand there are a mass of superfluous words like the articles. That is to say, English isn't a convenient language for the play which I am accustomed to. What can you write in that clumsy language apart from letters? (Sokolov c, p. 198).

Writers are concerned that separation from spoken Russian will adversely affect their work:

It's most difficult of all in emigration for writers who find themselves outside the borders of the motherland at a young age, when they're twenty or thirty. They encounter really serious problems, and they're the ones who have to think most often about changing the language they write in, about changing in the end to English, French or German . . .

I left the Soviet Union when I was already forty-eight. At that age it's already impossible to forget the language . . .

Although of course it's difficult sometimes, and you start feeling the lack of the Russian language keenly. At first I got particularly tired just from the sounds of the foreign language that surround you from morning to evening, from the advertisements, the shop signs written in foreign letters. Now that has passed.

By the way, that was when I especially fell in love with Chekhov again. There's someone whose Russian is really genuine, amazingly pure (Voinovich f, p. 131).

[Interviewer] Does the fact that a writer lives abroad influence his language in any way?
[S] Of course it does. For some people it's a whole drama. I know

writers who've stopped writing. They need living material in order to write, the language of the streets, and you don't get that here. Such a problem doesn't exist for me, because I write 'out of my head'. (Siniavskii a)

In Vienna I kept having this terrible dream that I had forgotten or was forgetting my language. Every time I caught myself making a linguistic error, I got worried: that's it, it's started (Sokolov c, p. 198).

. . . my literary fate would have been more fruitful in Russia, because here you lose the linguistic atmosphere (after all, a prose writer lives only in language). Language is a constantly developing organism. It gets old quickly, changes. You have to live in your own country and sense that in the social context. In that sense I have lost a lot (Maksimov a, p. 82).

The Russian language and Russia invariably remain their inspiration:

Even if I speak good French and German, all the same they're crutches, because I can't think in that language, I can't love that language the way I love Russian. So that in the cultural sense also I can't get completely accustomed to things, and probably no one can (Goricheva a).

It is the greatest happiness to see this land, to hear this extraordinary, great language, one of the greatest languages in the world. You understand yourself what language is for a man, for a people, it's the cipher of their thought. Whatever the crisis, Russia has remained Russia and that is the main thing for us (Mamleev a).

I never have thought of myself outside of Russian culture (Korzhavin e, p. 46).

My mother is there, my friends. Childhood memories link me to Russia. Those people, the people close to me who have remained there, will always be nearer to me than the people I have met here (Kuper a).

People ask me if I feel at home in the West. I reply that the friends I have made here, and there are lots of them in all corners of the world, cannot replace my old friends. I am swimming in an ocean of human relationships, and neither in Paris nor in Lucerne nor in New York have they been able to become for me the human hearth that Moscow was for many years (Kremer b, p. 46).

It's impossible to cut me off from Russia . . . I live through all its ups and all its downs, and when things are going badly for my country, I suffer, when it is soaring, I rejoice with it (Shemiakin a).

Here, in France, I have felt myself to be precisely a Russian artist, and I particularly wish to note that I am very very Russian . . . Working in Paris, it seems to me that I feel the way Gogol' did when he was writing *Dead Souls* in Rome. The best place to paint Russian pictures is precisely Paris. Why? Because you suddenly find yourself to be alien, in an unfamiliar situation, and you feel all of Russia in a different way, your sense of it is sharper; from here it seems to be very naive, strange, to exist behind a great Russian wall (Tselkov a, p. 11).

I have always remained a Russian patriot. Especially here in America. Believe me, the easiest thing of all would be to forget, to wash your hands of it, to start a new life . . . That's so much easier. But to remain Russian – that takes effort. And I want Aleksandr to grow up Russian, even though his mother is American. Here in America, being a prince is not a privilege, it's a burden. With every word, gesture, action, I am responsible here not only for myself but for my family [*za rod*], and . . . for the people [*za narod*]. You must do nothing that would give anyone reason to say gloatingly: look what those Russians are like! (Prince Volkonskii a)

Russia is also their primary audience. In the words of Nina Berberova: 'Who have I been working for all my life? It wasn't for Japanese and Brazilians.'[10]

We haven't been a great success in the West, we haven't become famous bestselling authors here. And we probably never will. It's the Russian reader who likes us, and we belong to the Russian reader (Aksenov k, p. 15).

The West has remained alien to me. And everything I did in terms of publishing activity and organising exhibitions I did and do more for those who have remained here. If the books and catalogues didn't come here, to Russia, I simply wouldn't have got involved in it (Glezer c).

When I argue with some of my colleagues I advance the following thesis: there are some very good writers here [in the West, JG], but *literature* is there! Literary life is there, and most important of all, the reader is there! And you can't get away from that (Kopelev a, p. 43).

There's no collective reader in the West (Korzhavin d, p. 168).

I paid little attention to my successes in France and America, because Russian success would be the real one (Odoevtseva d, p. 22).

I live for Russia and Russian culture. And all our affairs basically centre on Russia (Siniavskii in Siniavskii and Rozanova a).

I won't say that he [Vladimov's 'Ruslan', JG] is offended by the success he's had in the West . . . but all this can't be compared with the open and wide access to readers who are his fellow countrymen, to whom this tale was first addressed (Vladimov b).

Who is it all orientated to? 100% to a Russian reader, living above all in the USSR. And I don't intend to re-orientate myself . . . I tore myself away from the country with my blood, all my pain has remained here [i.e. in Russia, JG] (Voinovich d).

Even a professional maverick like Limonov says substantially the same thing:

Fortunately I've never been a Soviet writer.
[Interviewer] Why 'fortunately'?
[L] Because I have my own image of the 'Soviet writer'. He's a fat bourgeois uncle, who's making a career in literature. For me Solzhenitsyn is also a Soviet writer . . .
. . . Nevertheless I do consider myself a Soviet person, it's not for nothing that I say 'my father', 'my family' . . . I rebelled against them, but I'm still part of their flesh and blood . . .
. . . I think that what is being written now in Soviet papers

has made dissidence irrelevant and émigré publications meaningless . . .
[Interviewer] And would you like your novels to be published in the Soviet Union?
Of course, of course, after all, it's my people (Limonov a).

VI

In the emotionally heightened context of these interviews, the question of returning to live in Russia is frequently raised, often in the form of a ritual final question. Responses to it are various:

If they say to me tomorrow: 'Nikolai, come and settle in Moscow or in a suburb of the capital', I shall go without fail (Grand Duke Nikolai Romanovich Romanov a).

The place of a Russian writer now is here, I don't even understand how people can go away at this time. It doesn't matter at all what precisely happens, but undoubtedly it will be something tragic and lofty. The cause of civilisation and culture is pretty helpless. But we are directed to save it independently of our intentions. And that will happen precisely here . . . there is no other place so destined for passions of the most ardent kind. I want to be here and to see it (Sokolov b).

[Interviewer] What will help you to overcome the blows of fate?
[L] A breath of Moscow air. Although I have contractual duties in the West, I am speeding home, to the Taganka (Liubimov b, p. 42, last sentence).[11]

[Interviewer] Iurii Petrovich, would you like to return for good? You are ours [*Vy – nash*] and you ought to be in Moscow.
[L] You asked the question and you answered it yourself. I have nothing to add (Liubimov d, p. 4, last sentence).

Most people are more equivocal, and even express a certain irritation at the question:

I don't think that now I'll return to Russia for good, abandoning all my affairs here, my life 'here'. I just can't do that. I have a house here, permanent work, my students, literary affairs, theatrical and television projects . . .

. . . It's very important to me now to re-establish my links with Russia itself. I want to travel, to have a good close look at what is going on in Gorbachev's Rus', and maybe even sit down and do a bit of writing. And I don't rule out that when we get old it may be worth retiring a bit closer to our native hearth (Aksenov k, p. 15).

I can't say that when I came to Moscow I had the feeling of coming home . . . the house in Sokol'niki where I was born no longer exists . . .

I would always be ready to return. But in the first place no one is inviting me . . .

Besides . . . The children must finish their schooling . . . (Maksimov c).

Many directors are now getting the chance to work abroad. And that is normal. It's normal when they don't ask you 'Will you return?' (Mikhalkov-Konchalovskii a, p. 6).

[Interviewer] So would you return if you were invited?
[V.K.R.] Under certain conditions. Concretely, if the country stops being Communist (Grand Duke Vladimir Kirillovich Romanov b).

It seems completely unimportant to me where a writer's body is registered, and when I get asked about returning I say 'let my books return' (Siniavskii in Siniavskii and Rozanova c).

I don't even know how to reply. You know, the whole way you've put the question strikes me as artificial. Why doesn't anyone ask Graham Greene, an English writer living in France, whether he would like to return to England? If he wants to, he'll pay a visit . . . No one asked Hemingway 'will you return to America soon?' (Siniavskii in Siniavskii and Rozanova f, p. 29).[12]

It's not a matter of physical return. You can pay a visit to Russia or even return there for good while remaining alien to her and following egoistic aims. Or you can not go back while remaining her true son . . . The problem of my return to the Motherland is above all a problem for the Motherland herself and only in the last place for me personally (Zinov'ev b).

And some people are unequivocally certain that they will not return permanently:

I don't know about other people, but I myself will never return to the Soviet Union. My professional life has been formed here. In Paris in eight years I've painted about fifteen times as many paintings as I did in my entire life in Russia. How can I go away from myself? (Zaborov a).

I'll never return to the Soviet Union for good. In my time I have had several chats with consular bureaucrats. One of them asked me: 'Mariia Vasil'evna, now there's perestroika, don't you want to return?' I said no, I don't, I'm afraid. 'What d'you mean, Mariia Vasil'evna, afraid, the situation's different now.' 'No,' I said, 'I was never afraid of that. I'm afraid of something else. I'm afraid of dying of irritation. And d'you know why? The basic trouble with my Fatherland is that it's a colossal kindergarten. But I'm used to being an adult, I can't live in a kindergarten, where people forgot long ago how to make individual decisions' (Rozanova in Siniavskii and Rozanova f, p. 28).

The same irritation is expressed by Limonov:

[Interviewer] Haven't you had any sentimental feelings, any feeling of kinship?
[L] There are some old, repressed memories, but I can tell you honestly what I think: can I really have been born here? . . . can I really have been born in this country in which life is so inconvenient, with its constant tension? How did I live here? (Limonov b, p. 18).

Brodskii is not even sure that he can bear to make a visit:

[Interviewer] I hope we'll see you in Russia soon.
I'll tell you honestly, I'm a little bit afraid of that. As for hope, the remarkable English thinker Francis Bacon said, 'Hope is a good breakfast, but it is a bad supper' (Brodskii b).

I don't know if I'm in a state to come as a tourist.
[Interviewer] Why as a tourist?
Well, how else? A guest is a tourist. That's one thing. And . . .
Liuba, I'm not a metronome. Swinging back and forth. I probably
won't do it. It's just that a human being moves only in one
direction (Brodskii c).

The question of nostalgia provokes a number of eloquent responses:

Strange as it may seem, I rather miss the *déclassé* street public. I
want to chat to taxi drivers, ex-footballers, blokes I don't know in
the places where they drink beer. If they still drink it. Go to a
shashlyk bar. That free male Moscow, which still exists, I think,
they're the people I'd like to see (Aksenov j, p. 58).

Nostalgia? What can you say about it? What is it? A renunciation
of the demands of reality? I always tried to behave responsibly, not
to give in to sentimentality . . . I don't know if I've had a dose of
nostalgia or not. All I do know is that sometimes I felt that it was
essential to be in a specific place . . . that was impossible, and that
grieved me . . . I don't know if the thing I get is nostalgia (Brodskii
a, p. 29).[13]

In these years I have realised how difficult things are for me
without Russia. Nostalgia has set in. Nothing romantic, the most
genuine physiological nostalgia – I've simply started to suffocate
without Russia. Thank God *perestroika* started in time, and after
my fifth attempt they've finally let me in (Goricheva a).

Our nostalgia is a natural reaction to the foul abnormality of the
political and social situation. It's the same nostalgia felt by German
writers who left for France without any hope of ever returning to
the Motherland (Neizvestnyi e, p. 73).

I can only say one thing: of course there's nostalgia, the way any
Russian feels it, nostalgia for my youth, that's the finest thing we
have in life, nostalgia for my friends, who are beyond price, some
of whom have already left this fragile earth, some, fortunately, live
alongside me. Nostalgia for one of the most beautiful cities in the
world, Petersburg (*Piter*). But I don't feel any nostalgia for my

district policeman or my 38 neighbours: with one toilet for the lot of them, like in the Vysotskii song, or for the humiliations that fell to my lot, or for the Skvortsov-Stepanov clinic where they treated me for my enthusiasm for modernism and religion, or for the psychiatric clinic where I had forced treatment . . . I really do love Russia, but I love my new home too. And I just love wandering around the world, like any artist (Shemiakin e, p. 9).

. . . before I decided to leave, my life here had turned into such a nightmare that I have never had any nostalgia, I haven't felt sorry about what I left here, it was too horrific (Voinovich f, p. 133).

. . . the motherland is the motherland. I have thought about returning. It's important for me as a writer. I pined for a mother-land which didn't exist. I never pined for the country I'd left behind. I didn't pine for Brezhnev, or for the portraits of members of the Politburo, or for the policemen who stood and still stand on the streets in large numbers (Voinovich g, p. 48).

When I stayed behind in the West, for several years I refused to meet Russians, to read Russian books, to stop 'Nostalgia Iva-novna' eating away at me. I was always interested in the West. I wanted to stay and I didn't want to, my conscience got in the way, there was something scratching away at me. But there wasn't any dilemma . . . Probably when I'm old and I've nothing to do I'll start remembering and crying over Russia (Nuriev a, p. 21).[14]

Do I feel nostalgia? Does it torment me? Nostalgia is a sickness. I feel no nostalgia for birch trees (there are plenty of them in the world). For me it's not a geographical concept, it's a historical one. An ache about the past, when we were young and could have done a great deal . . . and did do a great deal . . . Remembering that is painful . . . But otherwise . . . No, not nostalgia . . . (Panich a, p. 25).

VII

It is possible that the heyday of the émigré interview in the Soviet press has passed, and it will come to be seen as a stage in their literary reclamation, like the publications of their writings. Certainly there are some signs that not all Soviet listeners are prepared to hang on their every word. There recently appeared in the independent Moscow journal *Panorama*, under the untranslatable epigraph from Daniil Kharms 'T'fu, mat'! . . .', a healthily and amusingly disrespectful description of an appearance at the Central House of Literature in Moscow by 'the legendarily unknown figure' of the émigré writer Iurii Mamleev. The 'leading surrealist of contemporary Russian literature, the idol of the Moscow underground of the early 80s', turns out to look like:

> the epitome of a regional level party (Soviet, trade union) worker. The same grey suit and darker tie . . . the same porridge [*kasha*] in his mouth. A grey quiff on his forehead gives him a passing resemblance to Ligachev.
>
> As is required at a surrealist evening, the chairman, the writer Vladimir Makanin, is absent. The reason for his absence is given briefly but incomprehensibly: 'He left and didn't come back.' Where did he go? What does 'didn't come back' mean? God knows . . .

A substitute chairman is found. Mamleev 'mumbles' his story 'Flight' 'in the voice of a mediocre schoolboy'. The story is lousy, Soviet editors have stories like it piled up in the corners of their offices. 'Waves of sleep and despondency spread through the hall.' When it comes to question time people perk up, passing severely practical questions to the leading surrealist: '"How did you manage to leave?", "Who paid for your ticket to the USA?", "Who looked after you in New York until you got a job?" . . . "Do émigré journals still take manuscripts from Russia?"' When Mamleev explains that in the West people don't really give a damn about literature and culture, especially émigré literature, 'a mood of patriotism begins to be felt in the hall'.

Then an 'unknown Mamleev scholar' passes the writer a voluminous study of the 'poetics, aesthetics and philosophy' of his novels and requests an audience. 'It was clear that this terrified him and he wanted to run as far away as possible, that it was only extraordinary strength of will that was keeping him on stage. . . .'

As surrealism requires, the conclusion of the evening is phantasmagorical:

'Hey!', the chairman suddenly rouses himself. 'What are we up to . . . what's on today at 9.40?'
'Kashpiro-o-o-ovskii' [a phenomenally popular hypnotist, JG], the hall bleats discordantly.
'Right!' says the chairman weightily. 'Well, then, let us thank Iurii Vital'evich . . .'[15]

In two of the most recent interviews considered here, both carried by the magazine *Ogonek* in the summer of 1990, a new subject is raised. The émigré actor and director Iulian Panich has spoken eloquently of emigration as a matter of life and death, and of not having the right to encourage other people to do so. His young interviewer nevertheless insists:

All the same. Would you advise me or representatives of my generation to leave?
[P] Yes. Unambiguously. Go. Establish yourself in that accursed world. You must work out from your own experience where it's best.
   The one thing you shouldn't do is to burn your bridges. Get yourself a passport for five years (it isn't so expensive). And then take a whirl in that society where nobody helps anybody (Panich a, p. 25).

The same subject arises in an extended interview with Iurii Liubimov which appeared two weeks later, and which is punctuated by the interviewer's repeated question, 'Was it worth coming back?' Eventually an exasperated Liubimov replies:

I've come back, and you're having an exodus. One person has returned and tens of thousands are making a run for it. From the fear, from the hopelessness, from the lies, I don't know. They lied for four years about Chernobyl', it's all clean, it's all safe. During that time hundreds of thousands paid with their health, and will go on to pay with their deaths, their infertility, their deformed children. The number of victims is like in a war. And no one is guilty. And those who lied are now 'taking measures'. They're lying so as not to lose their [special] rations, so as to go on eating sweetly. And no one has said to them, 'you're cannibals, quit your posts'. But these aren't Brezhnevite lies, which we're fed up of hearing about, these are today's lies. Once again the authorities are deceiving the people. Nothing changes . . . (Liubimov e, p. 28)

These words provoke a bitter postscript from his interviewer, Aleksandr Minkin:

We write and write about the need to give the exiles back their citizenship, the need to apologise to them. But it's probably not magazines who must do that, but the government. And for three years already they seem to be paying no heed. They're obviously busy.

But while we're talking about the return of the exiles, and the government isn't talking about them, hundreds of thousands are leaving, no, fleeing from the country. And no one does anything to stop them. Only the Supreme Soviet holds back the exodus a little by not passing an emigration law. But what will happen when it does pass it? That very day millions will be able to surge away. Just as 'unexpectedly' as they surged over the shelves of Ryzhkov's shops.

So what will happen, will we again call millions of citizens traitors to the Motherland? Just as we gave this criminal appellation to millions of soldiers who were taken prisoner for the same reason, the hopeless incompetence of the government?

And the fugitives won't be the worst sons of Russia, as they weren't the worst of the soldiers. It's not the idiots and the cripples, the old, the ill and the bureaucrats who'll leave the house, they'll all stay with us. It's the strong, practical, educated, energetic, honourable and hardworking who'll leave, the others wouldn't make a go of it, it's no paradise . . .

. . . I've been speaking to a quicktempered old man, who's seen everything and been through everything . . . I've been tormenting him with unpleasant questions, and he torments me by evading my questions, as he puts it, 'like a boxer dodging the punches'. And he's right. Because how long can we go on pretending that we're asking questions and forcing people to pretend that they're answering? Everyone knows everything, and we're sick of talking, sick of pretending . . . (Liubimov e, p. 29).

Are the new émigrés, as Panich hopes, a sign of the fabled 'normalisation' of the country, able to come and go at will? Or are they, as Minkin fears, the healthy abandoning a disaster zone, the 'fourth wave' of a despairingly repeated cycle? Only time will tell.

NOTES

1. See, for example, E.I. Zamiatin, *Povesti. Rasskazy* (Voronezh, 1986); V. Nabokov, 'Zashchita Luzhina', *Moskva*, 1986, 12, pp. 66–163.
2. This letter was repeatedly a bone of contention when signatories such as Aksenov and Liubimov were later interviewed in the Soviet press. They were not, however, disposed to recant.
3. For a more detailed survey of the 'return of the émigrés', see pp. 117–20 and 143–5; 136–8; and 156–7 of my 'The Literary Press', in *Culture and the Media in the USSR Today* (ed. Julian Graffy and Geoffrey A. Hosking) (London, 1989) pp. 107–57.
4. The list of 159 interviews with sixty-six émigrés at the end of this study does not aspire to completeness. I should like to take the opportunity to thank Martin Dewhirst of the University of Glasgow for supplying me with many of the pieces discussed here. It should be noted that the views of non-émigré artists and writers are also actively solicited through interviews and columns in Soviet newspapers and magazines.
5. The interviewees were Siniavskii, Vladimov, Voinovich, Korzhavin and Zinov'ev (*Inostrannaia literatura*, 1989, 2, pp. 240–50); and Aksenov, Etkind, Kopelev, Orlova, Odoevtseva, Sokolov, Dovlatov and Tsvetkov (ibid., 1989, 3, pp. 238–49).
6. As the editor of the leading émigré journal *Kontinent*, Maksimov was regularly described as the most virulently anti-Communist and anti-Soviet of émigrés. Thus he was among the last to be approached by Soviet interviewers. The first of these, Anna Pugach, describes the process of reclamation thus:

> When I got back to Moscow, I went to the bibliographical office of the Central House of Writers (the TsDL) which holds the fullest card index of writers. I could not find the name of Maksimov in the basic collection. 'His time hasn't come yet', said one of the women working there, taking out of the special collection (*spetskhran*) an already familiar wooden drawer with the word 'Emigrés' written on it, a drawer that had once been marked for destruction, but which someone had been good enough to preserve.
> Only six months ago it was quite heavy and close packed with the personal cards of Viktor Nekrasov, Vladimir Voinovich, Andrei Siniavskii, Vasilii Aksenov, Anatolii Gladilin, Lev Kopelev. Now it was empty. There was only one pile of cards left – the magazine, newspaper and literary publications of V. Maksimov, with a note at the end of the list: 'Abroad since 1973' (*Iunost'*, 1989, 12, p. 80).

7. Interviewed in the Riga newspaper *Atmoda* of 5 February 1990, Iurii Kublanovskii was asked to discuss Solzhenitsyn's 'absolute silence with regard to present day events in the USSR'.

He replied: 'Solzhenitsyn considers that he must first appear in Russia through his books. Besides, he is convinced that after so many years of exile he does not have the right to get involved in socio-journalistic processes, since this is a subtle matter, complicated by a mass of different additional factors. Solzhenitsyn does not want to miss the target; when he writes, he always wants to "hit the target".'
Solzhenitsyn's 'Kak nam obustroit' Rossiiu. Posil'nye soobrazheniia' (How we are to rebuild Russia. Considerations within my power') appeared in *Komsomol'skaia pravda*, pp. 3–6 on 18 September 1990, and in *Literaturnaia gazeta*, pp. 3–6 on the same day. It was also published as a supplement to the émigré newspaper *Russkaia mysl'*, 3846, 21 September 1990.

8. There are many examples of this: we note, for example Aksenov (b), Maksimov (a), Neizvestnyi (e), Ratushinskaia (a), Gavrilov (b) and several interviews with Voinovich.
9. Aksenov refers frequently in his interviews to the campaign against him in the journal *Krokodil* in 1988; Siniavskii and Rozanova to the failure to give them entry visas in time for them to attend the funeral of Iulii Daniel'. In the same vein, Voinovich writes with withering anger about his treatment by Soviet bureaucrats during his recent visit to Moscow to discuss having his novel *Zhizn' i neobychainye prikliucheniia soldata Ivana Chonkina* filmed by El'dar Riazanov at Mosfil'm. See V. Voinovich, 'Otrezannyi lomot'', *Ogonek*, 1989, 43, pp. 7–8.
   A last big group of émigrés, including Solzhenitsyn, Aksenov, Voinovich, Vladimov and Ratushinskaia, finally got their Soviet citizenship back (if they wanted it) by a presidential decree of 15 August 1990. See, for example, *Russkaia mysl'*, 3842, 24 August 1990, p. 2.
10. Quoted by E. Lubiannikova in the introduction to chapters from N. Berberova, 'Kursiv moi', *Oktiabr'* 1988, 10, p. 164.
11. Compare 'When I saw the reception arranged for me at Ben Gurion airport, I felt that I was home, with my family and friends.' (Liubimov's press conference on his return from the Taganka to Israel: '*Russkaia mysl'*, 3731, 1 July 1988, p. 11, last sentence).
12. A similar point is made repeatedly in interviews by Vasilii Aksenov.
13. In the émigré journal *Strana i mir*, 1988, 3, Brodskii told Tomas Venclova: 'I don't feel nostalgia for the motherland as such. For Leningrad, yes.'
14. These remarks provoke a postscript from the interviewer: 'We shouldn't console ourselves with illusions that they'll return. It's hardly likely: they're not prodigal sons.'
15. Extracted from V. Nikov, 'Zhivoi Mamleev', *Panorama*, Moscow, 11, 1989, reprinted in *Russkaia mysl'*, 3808, 5 January 1990, p. 11. This article provoked an angry protest from Aleksandr Glezer and a spirited defence from a representative of *Panorama*: see *Russkaia mysl'*, 3812, 26 January 1990, p. 13.

INTERVIEWS WITH ÉMIGRÉS IN THE SOVIET PRESS:
SELECTED BIBLIOGRAPHY

Aksenov, Vasilii (writer)

(a) [Otvety na anketu], *Inostrannaia literatura*, 1989, 3, pp. 238–9.
(b) '"Ia, po suti dela, ne emigrant . . ."', *Iunost'*, 1989, 4, pp. 80–3.
(c) 'V poiskakh grustnogo bebi', *Skif*, 1989, 6, [unnumbered pp.]
(d) 'Ia nikogda ne byl antisovetchikom', *Novoe vremia*, 48, 1989, p. 46.
(e) 'Zhal', chto Vas ne bylo s nami v eto vremia', *Moskovskie novosti*, 1989, 48, p. 28.
(f) 'Aksenov's Distance', *Moskovskii komsomolets*, 10 December 1989, pp. 10–11.
(g) '"Vozniklo oshchushchenie zhivoi strany"', *Sobesednik*, 1989, 50, p. 10.
(h) '"Vzgliad na nas i na sebia"', *Avrora*, 1990, 1, pp. 86–90.
(i) 'Pravo na svoi ostrov', *Ogonek*, 1990, 2, pp. 18–19.
(j) '"Ia v osnovnom pishu dlia russkikh chitatelei . . ."', *Iskusstvo kino*, 1990, 3, pp. 51–60.
(k) 'Ostaius' russkim pisatelem', *Nedelia*, 1990, 35, pp. 3, 15.

Alloi, Vladimir (publisher)

(a) '"Minuvshee" i vek nyneshnii', *Nedelia*, 1990, 7, pp. 22–3.

Ashkenazy, Vladimir (musician)

(a) '"Ne liubliu byt' v tsentre vnimaniia"', *Novoe vremia*, 1989, 47, pp. 46–7.

Baianova, Alla (singer)

(a) 'Mechta Ally Baianovoi', *Novoe vremia*, 1989, 23, p. 48.
(b) 'Nizko klaniaius' tsyganam', *Novoe vremia*, 1989, 25, p. 48.

Berberova, Nina (writer)

(a) 'Ne tol'ko kursiv', *Literaturnaia gazeta*, 1989, 20, p. 15.
(b) '"My uezzhali ne navsegda"', *Vechernii Leningrad*, 18 September 1989, p. 3.
(c) 'Byl li Trotskii Masonom?', *Smena*, Leningrad, 22 September 1989, p. 3.
(d) 'Legko mne zhit' sredi liudei', *Knizhnoe obozrenie*, 1989, 35, pp. 8–9.
(e) '"Ne proshlo i semidesiati let . . ."', *Literaturnoe obozrenie*, 1990, 2, pp. 68–73.

Bobyshev, Dmitrii (writer)

(a) '"Ia uezzhal navsegda . . ."', *Sovetskaia kul'tura*, 7 November 1989, p. 6.

Brodskii, Iosif (writer)

(a) 'Cheloveka mozhno vsegda spasti', *Ogonek*, 1988, 30, pp. 28–9.
(b) 'Stokgol'm. Dekabr'. 1987', *Iunost'*, 1988, 8, p. 66.
(c) '"Ia – kochevnik"', *Skif*, 1989, 9, [unnumbered pp.].
(d) '"Ia vsegda oshchushchal sebia svobodnym . . ."', *Studencheskii meridian*, 1989, 10, pp. 49–51 [Translated from *Vogue*].
(e) 'Beseda Amandy Aizpuriete s Iosifom Brodskim', *Rodnik*, 1990, 3, pp. 72–3.
(f) 'Sud'ba strany mne daleko ne bezrazlichna', *Nedelia*, 1990, 9, p. 22.

Chagall, Valentina (widow of Marc Chagall)

(a) '"Kak on byl by schastliv!"', *Literaturnaia gazeta*, 1987, 36, p. 14.

Chalidze, Valerii (writer and publisher)

(a) 'Prizvanie sotsial'nyi kritik', *Moskovskie novosti*, 1989, 18, p. 16.

Dovlatov, Sergei (writer)

(a) [Otvety na anketu], *Inostrannaia literatura*, 1989, 3, pp. 246–7.
(b) 'Ia vstretilsia s pisatelem Sergeem Dovlatovym v N'iu-Iorke', *Nedelia*, 1990, 3, p. 23.
(c) 'Dar organicheskogo bezliubiia', *Ogonek*, 1990, 24, pp. 28–9.

Etkind, Efim (literary critic)

(a) [Otvety na anketu], *Inostrannaia literatura*, 1989, 3, pp. 239–42.

Fedorova, Viktoriia (actress)

(a) '"I reside in the United States, but my soul is here in Moscow"', *Soviet Film*, 1990, 6, pp. 24–5.
(b) 'Sud'ba Zoi Fedorovoi', *Argumenty i fakty*, 1990, 35, p. 6 (extracted from an interview which first appeared in A. Mirchev, *15 interv'iu*, New York, 1989, pp. 177–201).

Feodosiia, Mother (Orthodox nun)

(a) 'Russkaia obitel'' na kholmakh Burgundii', *Nedelia*, 1990, 31, p. 12.

Gavrilov, Andrei (pianist)

(a) 'Kak prosnut'sia znamenitym?', *Novoe vremia*, 1989, 37, pp. 40–1.
(b) Chuvstvo otvoevannoi svobody', *Ogonek*, 1989, 49, pp. 5–7, 26–9.

Glezer, Aleksandr (art critic and publisher)

(a) 'Nuzhen muzei sovremennogo russkogo iskusstva', *Iskusstvo*, 1989, 5, pp. 34–8.

(b) 'Iskusstvo ne dolzhno byt' v emigratsii', *Moskovskie novosti*, 1989, 5, p. 11.
(c) '"Politika somknulas' s nostal'giei"', *Novoe vremia*, 1990, 11, p. 48.

Goricheva, Tat'iana (writer)

(a) 'Ne stat' fariseiami stradaniia', *Smena*, Leningrad, 25 January 1990.

Ianov, Aleksandr (political scientist)

(a) 'Nuzhno sperva vyzhit', *Knizhnoe obozrenie*, 1990, 26, pp. 8–9.
(b) 'Reforma i kontrreforma', *Sovetskaia kul'tura*, 9 June 1990, p. 14.

Kalik, Mikhail (film director)

(a) '"Liubit' . . ." vospreshchaetsia', *Sovetskii ekran*, 1990, 3, p. 5.

Kerenskii, Gleb (son of Aleksandr Kerenskii)

(a) '"Sud'by skreshcheniia". Vstrecha s synom Kerenskogo', *Nedelia*, 1989, 30, pp. 10–11.

Kibal'chik, Vladimir ('Vladi', painter)

(a) 'Kibal'chik, syn Kibal'chika', *Nedelia*, 1990, 23, pp. 14–15.

Kopelev, Lev (writer)

(a) 'Razluka', *Novoe vremia*, 1988, 44, pp. 42–3.
(b) [Otvety na anketu], *Inostrannaia literatura*, 1989, 3, pp. 242–3.

Koreneva, Elena (actress)

(a) 'Ia ne byla gonimoi emigrantkoi', *Skif*, 1989, 5, [unnumbered pp.].

Korzhavin, Naum (writer)

(a) [Otvety na anketu], *Inostrannaia literatura*, 1989, 2, pp. 247–9.
(b) 'U nas net prava na pessimizm', *Moskovskie novosti*, 1989, 7, p. 16.
(c) 'Zhizn' pod diktovku stikhov', *Sovetskaia Estoniia*, 3 March 1989, p. 2.
(d) 'Garmoniia protiv bezvremen'ia', *Voprosy literatury*, 1989, 7, pp. 166–82.
(e) 'Ne priemliu ekstremizma', *Novoe vremia*, 1989, 18, p. 46.
(f) '"Segodnia nado dumat' ne o tom, kak «probivat'» rukopisi, a o tom, kak pisat'"', *Knizhnoe obozrenie*, 1989, 21, p. 10.

Kremer, Gidon (violinist)

(a) 'Vozvrashchenie', *Ogonek*, 1989, 34, pp. 20–1.

(b) 'Gidon Kremer i ego "komanda"', *Novoe vremia*, 1989, 43, pp. 46–7.
(c) 'Vernite muzyku', *Novoe vremia*, 1990, 3, p. 39.

Kublanovskii, Iurii (writer)

(a) 'S pozitsii khristianina v istorii', *Atmoda*, Riga, 5 February 1990.
(b) 'Ne otrekaiutsia, liubia', *Komsomol'skaia pravda*, 18 February 1990, p. 4.

Kuper, Iurii (painter)

(a) '"Malen'kie tragedii" Iuriia Kupera', *Nedelia*, 1989, 37, p. 19.

Liepa, Andris (ballet dancer)

(a) 'Ia podozhdu . . .' *Ogonek*, 1990, 6, infix + p. 17.

Limonov, Eduard (writer)

(a) 'Eto on, Edichka', *Moskovskie novosti*, 1989, 32, p. 16.
(b) 'Dialog s "normal'nym pisatelem"', *Ogonek*, 1990, 7, pp. 18–19.
(c) '"Ia khochu umeret' molodym"', *Knizhnoe obozrenie*, 21, 1990, pp. 8–9.
(d) 'Eta strana uviazla v nigilizme', *Dom kino*, 1990, 1, pp. 3–4.

Liubimov, Iurii (theatre director)

(a) 'Vstrecha', *Moskovskie novosti*, 1988, 21, p. 14.
(b) '"Domoi, na Taganku"', *Novoe vremia*, 1988, 46, pp. 42–3.
(c) 'Zhizn' prozhita vmeste', *Novoe vremia*, 1989, 7, p. 46.
(d) 'Dazhe demokratiia ne daet prava na raznuzdannost'', *Dom kino*, 1989, 5, pp. 3–4.
(e) 'Kabala sviatosh', *Ogonek*, 1990, 27, pp. 8, 26–9.

L'vov, Arkadii (writer)

(a) 'Bol'shoe solntse Odessy', *Nedelia*, 1989, 35, p. 20.

Makarova, Natal'ia (ballet dancer)

(a) 'Na rodnoi zemle', *Moskovskie novosti*, 1989, 6, p. 2.
(b) 'Dvadtsat' let spustia', *Novoe vremia*, 1989, 9, p. 48.

Maksimov, Vladimir (writer)

(a) 'V gostiakh u «Kontinenta»', *Iunost'*, 1989, 12, pp. 80–4.
(b) '"Nado priznat'sia, vse my zhertvy"', *Knizhnoe obozrenie*, 1990, 14, pp. 8–9.
(c) 'Vsegda i vezde ostaius' rossiianinom', *Moskovskaia pravda*, 25 April 1990, p. 3.

(d) 'Nuzhno obshchenatsional'noe primirenie', *Izvestiia*, 3 May 1990, p. 3.
(e) 'Ia zhivu Rossiei', *Golos rodiny*, 1990, 24, p. 13.

Mamleev, Iurii (writer)

(a) 'Vzgliad so storony', *Vecherniaia Moskva*, 21 October 1989, p. 3.

Mikhalkov-Konchalovskii, Andrei (Andrei Konchalovskii, film director)

(a) 'U menia vsegda byl bilet v Moskvu', *Argumenty i fakty*, 1988, 47, pp. 6–7.
(b) '"Ostaius' sovetskim"', *Ogonek*, 1989, 51, pp. 16–19.
(c) '"Uchit'sia terpimosti"', *Teatral'naia zhizn'*, 1989, 13, pp. 15–17.
(d) 'Tam i zdes'', *Sovetskii ekran*, 1990, 1, pp. 24–5.

Miller, Boris (publisher and member of NTS)

(a) 'Tot samyi NTS', *Argumenty i fakty*, 1990, 14, p. 4.

Neizvestnyi, Ernst (sculptor)

(a) 'Monument chelovecheskoi skorbi', *Moskovskie novosti*, 1988, 46, p. 7.
(b) 'Khudozhnik eto Gulliver', *Sovetskii ekran*, 1989, 10, p. 18.
(c) 'Drevo zhizni', *Novoe vremia*, 1989, 13, pp. 46–8.
(d) 'Mezhdu molotom i nakoval'nei', *Iskusstvo kino*, 1989, 6, pp. 61–2.
(e) '"Ia vsiudu odin i tot zhe"', *Druzhba narodov*, 1989, 12, pp. 63–81.
(f) '"Kul'tura – eto migratsiia liudei i idei"', *Sobesednik*, 1990, 28, p. 10.

Nekrich, Aleksandr (historian)

(a) 'SSSR: Istoriia i perestroika. Vzgliad iz-za okeana', *Moskovskie novosti*, 1989, 41, p. 10.
(b) '"Istoriia – tiazheloe moe remeslo"', *Sobesednik*, 1990, 11, p. 10.

Nuriev, Rudol'f (ballet dancer)

(a) 'Sootechestvennik', *Nedelia*, 1989, 21, pp. 20–1.
(b) 'Nuriev – na stsene Kirovskogo', *Izvestiia*, 12 November 1989, p. 3.
(c) '"Eto – schastlivoe vozvrashchenie"', *Novoe vremia*, 1989, 48, p. 47.

Odoevtseva, Irina (writer)

(a) 'Vstrechi s Gumilevym', *Nedelia*, 1988, 37, p. 18.
(b) 'Ozhivshie golosa', *Voprosy literatury*, 1988, 12, pp. 109–29.
(c) [Otvety na anketu], *Inostrannaia literatura*, 1989, 3, pp. 244–5.
(d) 'S voskhishcheniem zhivu', *Ogonek*, 1989, 11, pp. 22–3.

Orlova, Raisa (writer)

(a) 'Ia vstala k okoshku «dlia sovetskikh grazhdan» . . .', *Moskovskie novosti*, 1988, 43, p. 10.
(b) [Otvety na anketu], *Inostrannaia literatura*, 1989, 3, pp. 243–4.

Panich, Iulian (actor and director)

(a) '"Dvazhdy v odnu reku"', *Ogonek*, 1990, 25, pp. 23–5.

Ratushinskaia, Irina (writer)

(a) 'Togda sudili za stikhi', *Komsomol'skaia pravda*, 4 March 1990, p. 3.

Romanov, Grand Duke Nikolai Romanovich

(a) '"Perestroika – zalog mnogikh uspekhov"', *Nedelia*, 1990, 13, p. 15.

Romanov, Grand Duke Vladimir Kirillovich

(a) 'Korona russkoi imperii', *Ogonek*, 1990, 2, pp. 28–9.
(b) 'Pretendent na prestol', *Moskovskie novosti*, 1990, 31, p. 11.

Rostropovich, Mstislav and Vishnevskaia, Galina (musicians)

(a) '"My byli istinnymi soldatami russkoi muzyki"', *Argumenty i fakty*, 1990, 7, p. 6.

Sevela, Efraim (writer)

(a) '"Esli kto-nibud' zastrelit Gorbacheva, to eto budut liudi iz «Pamiati»"' *Kauno Aidas*, 28 September 1989, p. 2

Shakhovskaia, Zinaida (writer)

(a) '"Ne padaite dukhom, poruchik Golitsyn . . ."', *Dom kino*, 1989, 11, pp. 5–6, 12.
(b) '"My – deti Rossii"', *Knizhnoe obozrenie*, 1990, 10, pp. 8–9.

Shemiakin, Mikhail (painter)

(a) '"Menia otdelit' ot Rossii nevozmozhno . . ."', *Nedelia*, 1988, 38, p. 7.
(b) '"Kartina – eto dialog"', *Moskovskie novosti*, 1989, 13, p. 2.
(c) 'Iz plena . . .', *Novoe vremia*, 1989, 14, pp. 46–7.
(d) 'Khudozhnik igraet vedushchuiu rol'', *Knizhnoe obozrenie*, 1989, 14, p. 9.
(e) 'Svidanie s Rossiei', *Ogonek*, 1989, 23, pp. 8–10.

(f) 'Mikhail Shemiakin i Serzh Sorokko beseduiut s iskusstvovedom Vladimirom Tsel'tnerom', *Iskusstvo*, 1989, 8, pp. 52–6.

Shliapentokh, Vladimir (sociologist)

(a) '"Ia – za sotrudnichestvo"', *Sotsiologicheskie issledovaniia*, 1989, 6, pp. 106–11.

Siniavskii, Andrei and Rozanova, Mariia (writers)
[a, d and e, Siniavskii alone, i, Rozanova alone]

(a) '"Ia zhivu russkoi kul'turoi"', *Nedelia*, 1989, 1, p. 20.
(b) '"Tam my schitaemsia krasnymi"', *Knizhnoe obozrenie*, 1989, 2, p. 3.
(c) '"Emigratsiia – opyt strashnyi, no pouchitel'nyi"', *Moskovskie novosti*, 1989, 2, p. 16.
(d) [Otvety na anketu], *Inostrannaia literatura*, 1989, 2, pp. 241–3.
(e) 'Kakim ne dolzhen byt' pamiatnik', *Dekorativnoe iskusstvo*, 1989, 5, p. 18.
(f) 'Vsia zhizn'', *Teatral'naia zhizn'*, 1989, 14, pp. 28–31.
(g) 'Besedy s Andreem Siniavskim i Mariei Rozanovoi o Pushkine, i ne tol'ko o nem', *Knizhnoe obozrenie*, 1990, 4, pp. 8–9.
(h) 'Abrashka Terts, professor iz Sorbonny', *Literator*, Leningrad, 20 (25), 8 June 1990, pp. 4–5.
(i) 'Ne sotvori sebe kumira', *Studencheskii meridian*, 1990, 8, pp. 72–4.

Sokolov, Sasha (writer)

(a) [Otvety na anketu], *Inostrannaia literatura*, 1989, 3, pp. 245–6.
(b) 'Zhizn' nazyvalas'', *Skif*, 1989, 8, [unnumbered pp.].
(c) '"Vremia dlia chastnykh besed . . ."', *Oktiabr'*, 1989, 8, pp. 195–202.
(d) 'Amerikantsy ne mogut poniat' – o chem eto mozhno govorit' dva chasa', *Iunost'*, 1989, 12, pp. 66–7.

Tokarev, Villi (singer)

(a) '"Ia schastliv pet' na rodine . . ."', *Novoe vremia*, 1989, 23, p. 44.
(b) 'Posleslovie k odnim gastroliam', *Argumenty i fakty*, 1989, 39, p. 7.

Troitskaia, Natal'ia (singer)

(a) 'Dalekaia zvezda', *Novoe vremia*, 1989, 31, p. 48.

Tselkov, Oleg (painter)

(a) '"Ia nemnogo chuzhoi povsiudu"', *Nedelia*, 1989, 45, pp. 10–11.

Tsukerman, Slava (film director)

(a) 'Ia zhil v tsentre mira', *Skif*, 1989, 10, [unnumbered pp.].

Tsvetkov, Aleksei (writer)

(a) [Otvety na anketu], *Inostrannaia literatura*, 1989, 3, pp. 247–8.

Vishnevskaia, Galina (singer)

(a) 'Do vstrechi v Moskve', *Novoe vremia*, 1990, 5, p. 46.
(b) '"Rodinu daet nam Bog"', *Knizhnoe obozrenie*, 1990, 6, p. 7.

Vladimov, Georgii (writer)

(a) [Otvety na anketu], *Inostrannaia literatura*, 1989, 2, pp. 243–5.
(b) 'Tragediia Vernogo Ruslana', *Moskovskie novosti*, 1989, 4, p. 16.
(c) 'Russkii pisatel' v izgnanii', *Moskovskie novosti*, 1990, 23, p. 16.

Voinovich, Vladimir (writer)

(a) '"Ia vse eti gody zhil nadezhdoi . . ."', *Iunost'*, 1988, 10, pp. 81–3.
(b) [Otvety na anketu], *Inostrannaia literatura*, 1989, 2, pp. 245–7.
(c) 'Na pyl'nykh tropinkakh dalekikh planet . . .', *Sovetskii ekran*, 1989, 10, pp. 28–9.
(d) 'Vsia moia bol' ostaetsia zdes'', *Knizhnoe obozrenie*, 1989, 12, p. 4.
(e) 'Kak eto delalos'', *Iskusstvo kino*, 1989, 8, pp. 128–33.
(f) '"Staraius' sokhranit' sebia . . ."', *Teatr*, 1989, 8, pp. 129–34.
(g) '"A vy znaete, kakoi on?"', *Sovetskaia bibliografiia*, 1989, 4, pp. 43–9.
(h) 'S chego vse nachalos' . . .', *Studencheskii meridian*, 1989, 9, pp. 48–9.
(i) 'O moem neputevom bludnom syne', *Iunost'*, 1990, 1, pp. 76–8.

Volkonskii, Prince Oleg Valentinovich (translator)

(a) 'K Rossii, s liubov'iu. V gostiakh u O.V. Volkonskogo na Massachusets-Aveniu v Vashingtone', *Nedelia*, 1989, 43, p. 18.

von Fal'ts-Fein, Baron Eduard Aleksandrovich

(a) 'Ia ostalsia russkim . . .', *Moskovskie novosti*, 1989, 47, p. 16.

Zaborov, Boris (painter)

(a) 'Voskhozhdenie na parizhskii Olimp', *Nedelia*, 1990, 27, p. 15.

Zinov'ev, Aleksandr (writer)

(a) [Otvety na anketu], *Inostrannaia literatura*, 1989, 2, pp. 249–50.
(b) 'Ne krivil dushoi, ne prisposablivalsia . . .', *Moskovskie novosti*, 1989, 33, p. 16.
(c) 'Doza gor'kogo lekarstva. Tri vstrechi s Aleksandrom Zinov'evym', *Pravda*, 6 June 1990, p. 8.

Index

Entries are arranged in letter-by-letter order. Location references in bold type denote pages which contain quotations from authors or their works.

Trediakovskii, V., 62, 74
Troitskaia, N., 156
Trubetskoi, N.S., 28
Tselkov, O., **138**, 156
Tsiavlovskii, M.A., 26
Tsukerman, S., 156
Tsvetaeva, M., 18, 23–4 n.7
Türen öffen sich langsam, Die, **92**,
   94–5, **96–7**, 98, 99, 101 notes 1
   and 7, *see also* Orlova, R.
Turgenev, I.S., 91
Tvardovskii, A., 125

'Uezdnyi chudotvorets', *see* Shipov,
   I.
Universitetskaia poema, 17–18, *see
   also* Nabokov, V.
Uraniia, **39**, 40 n.2, *see also*
   Brodskii, I.

Vail', P., 82
'V Anglii', 19–20, 24–5, *see also*
   Brodskii, I.
'Three Knights', 20
'York', 20–3
Vasil'ev, B., 9
Vasil'ev, F.A., 31
'V avangarde – bez tylov', 50 *see
   also* Aksenov V.
Vernyi Ruslan, 139, *see also*
   Vladimov, G.
Vishnevskaia, G., 157
Vladimov, G., **124**, **125**, **139**, 149
   n.9, 157
Voinovich, V., 115, 117, **120–1**,
   123, **126–7**, **136**, **139**, **144**, 148
   n.6, 149 n.9, 157
Volkonskii, Prince O.V., **138**, 157

Von Fal'ts-Fein, Baron E.A., 157
'Vostok i Zapad', **105**, *see also*
   Zinov'ev, A.
V poiskakh grustnogo bebi, 50, 51,
   53–4, **55–6**, **57–9**, 60 notes 4,
   10 and 14, *see also* Aksenov,
   V.
V preddverii raiia, 103, 107, **108**,
   114   n.1, *see also* Zinov'ev, A.
Vyshinksii, A.Ia., 82
Vysotskii, V., 43, 144
'Vzgliad', 83

Wolfe, T., 46

Zaborov, B., **121**, **142**, 157
Zapiski nochnogo storozha, **106–7**,
   114 n.9, *see also* Zinov'ev, A.
Zatonskii, D., 117
Zavist', *see* Olesha, Iu.K.
Zhdanov, A.A., 98
Zheltyi dom, **104–5**, 106, 107,
   108–10, 114 n.3, *see also*
   Zinov'ev, A.
Ziiaiushchie vysoty, x, 102, 103,
   106, 110, 114 n.8, *see also*
   Zinov'ev, A.
Zinik, Z., x, xi, 12–16, 61 n.19
Zinov'ev, A., x, 56, 60 n.5, 61
   n.21, 117, **121–2**, **127**, **141–2**,
   148 n.5, 157
   and Soviet Union, 105–8
   and West, 102–5, 109–14
Zolotaia nasha zhelezka, 51, 60
   n.7, **61 n.22**, *see also* Aksenov,
   V.
Zoshchenko, M.M., 4